OKLAHOMA RENEGADES

OKLAHOMA RENEGADES
Their Deeds and Misdeeds

KEN BUTLER

PELICAN PUBLISHING COMPANY
Gretna 2000

First printing, October 1997
Second printing, July 2000

Library of Congress Cataloging-in-Publication Data

Butler, Ken.
    Oklahoma renegades : their deeds and misdeeds / Ken Butler.
        p.   cm.
    Includes bibliographical references and index.
    ISBN 1-56554-231-2 (pbk. : alk. paper)
        1. Outlaws—Oklahoma—Biography—Anecdotes. 2. Frontier and
    pioneer life—Oklahoma—Anecdotes. 3. Oklahoma—Biography-
    -Anecdotes.   I. Title.
    F699.B96 1997
    976.6'05'0922—dc20
                                                            96-44302
                                                                CIP

Manufactured in the United States of America

Published by Pelican Publishing Company, Inc.
1000 Burmaster Street, Gretna, Louisiana 70053

Contents

List of Illustrations

Preface

There has been much written about the noted lawmen and the notorious outlaws who operated in Oklahoma and Indian Territories. Mention of these subjects usually brings to mind the names of the better remembered lawmen such as Bill Tilghman, Heck Thomas, Chris Madsen, and the outlaw bands known as the Dalton, Doolin, Rufus Buck, and Bill Cook gangs, as well as infamous individuals such as Cherokee Bill and Henry Starr. While they are all worthy subjects, the events of their lives that have captured our interest have been well reported in numerous books and magazine articles.

To acquaint some of my friends who are interested in the history of Oklahoma lawmen and outlaws with a little known outlaw who had previously caught my interest, some time ago I decided to write an article for the *Oklahombres* quarterly about Bert Casey. Wanting to present the most complete and accurate article possible about this young desperado, I renewed my research into Bert Casey's short, violent life. In so doing, I soon became intrigued with the Hughes brothers and their "Outlaw Ranch On The Washita," where Casey hid out. As I delved deeper into the stories about Ben and Jim Hughes' many "brushes with the law," I became attracted to Fred Hudson, Lute Houston, Sam Baker, Willis Brooks, Dr. Zeno Beemblossom, attorney Moman Pruiett, and "Hookey" Miller.

Five years after starting my initial article about Bert Casey (during which time I drove thousands of miles and spent countless hours scanning old newspapers, researching records, and soliciting information from all the sources I thought might help, then spending untold days at my word processor), I finally completed what was originally intended to be a short, simple article. I hope that you, the reader, will enjoy my reporting of some of the events in the lives of these unique and forgotten men of early-day Oklahoma.

Consideration was given to including the term "Twin Territories" in the title of this book. I later decided that currently more people will visualize the actual area involved if simply termed "Oklahoma" rather than if the popular name of the region before statehood was applied to the two areas involved.

In my research I encountered numerous problems in locating information about certain periods in the lives of some of these subjects, and those years remain unaccounted for. I also learned that records needed to clarify the disposition of some criminal charges are not available. I became perplexed about whether to continue with what I could learn about the men involved, or simply to drop the project. I decided to continue and, in those cases, to acknowledge the lack of information and offer the logical assumptions. This course was chosen after accepting that in some instances when these subjects were alive the courts and officers involved obviously failed to cope with and account for some of their activities, and that time has but faded their dim trail of yesteryear. Another researcher may still uncover more complete information than I have found, or perhaps find answers to questions that may arise from this work.

I would like to express my gratitude to the many people who have provided information and helped in the assembly of this work. Among those who have done so are:

Anne Diestel, Federal Bureau of Prisons, Washington, DC; Bette Williams, Checotah, OK; Charles F. Loefke, Deputy Court Clerk, Lawton, OK; Charles Rainbolt, Stillwater, OK; Dale Willits, Lookeba, OK; Deanna Bonner, Court Clerk, Hobart,

OK; Debbie Riddle, Anadarko, OK; Edward Herring, Mt. Hope, AL; Frankie Shipman, Oklahoma City; Fred Hudson, Harrison, AR; Helen Gaines, San Angelo, TX; Jack Collier, Anadarko, OK; Jim Rabon, Oklahoma Department of Corrections, Oklahoma City; John Ross, Custer County State Bank, Arapaho, OK; Marion Smith, Oxford, England; Meg Hacker, Southwest Regional Archives, Fort Worth, TX; Mike Brown, Rock Springs, WY; Nancy Samuelson, Eastford, CT; Patty Davis, Fort Smith, AR; Phillip Steele, Springdale, AR; Richard Jones, Oklahoma City; R.L. Oaks, Canute, OK; Robert Ernst, Stillwater, OK; Susan Bradford, Duke, OK; Steve Bunch, Perry, OK; Ted Thompson, Carnegie, OK; Terry Whitehead, Blackwell, OK; my daughter Doris Tomlin, of Oklahoma City, who reviewed my writing and offered corrections; and, last but not least, my wife Maurine ("Rene"), who endorsed my efforts and the many hours that I have devoted to this project.

I may have failed to list some who have provided input, but I sincerely thank each one who has helped in my endeavor to gather the information and write this account of some of these colorful *Oklahoma Renegades.*

Ken Butler
Shawnee, Oklahoma

OKLAHOMA RENEGADES

Map #1

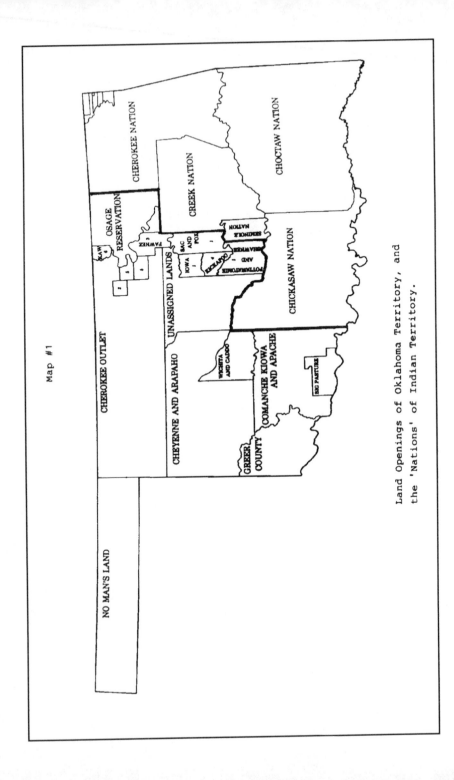

Land Openings of Oklahoma Territory, and
the 'Nations' of Indian Territory.

Map #2

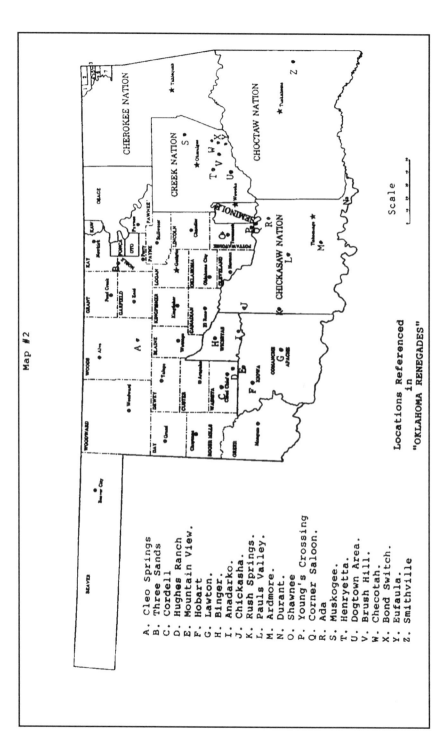

Locations Referenced
in
"OKLAHOMA RENEGADES"

A. Cleo Springs
B. Three Sands
C. Cordell
D. Hughes Ranch
E. Mountain View.
F. Hobart
G. Lawton.
H. Binger.
I. Anadarko.
J. Chickasha.
K. Rush Springs.
L. Pauls Valley.
M. Ardmore.
N. Durant.
O. Shawnee
P. Young's Crossing
Q. Corner Saloon.
R. Ada
S. Muskogee.
T. Henryetta.
U. Dogtown Area.
V. Brush Hill.
W. Checotah.
X. Bond Switch.
Y. Eufaula.
Z. Smithville

Scale

Map #3

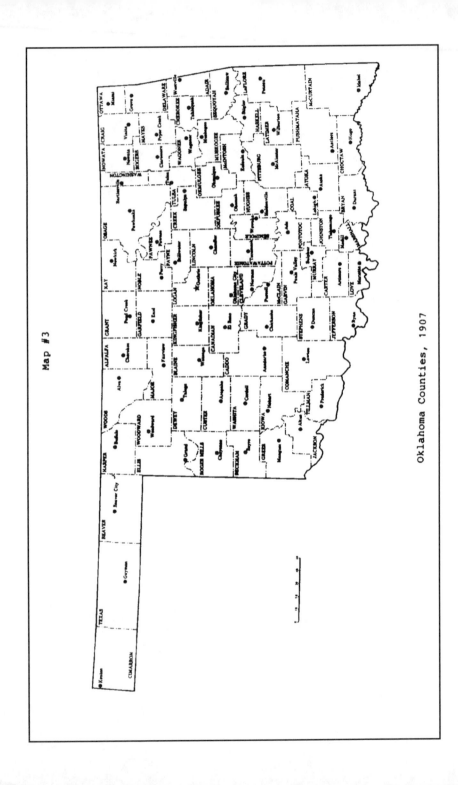

Oklahoma Counties, 1907

CHAPTER 1

A Train Robbery in Texas

On October 19, 1894, a section gang was working on the Texas and Pacific railway, three miles east of Gordon, Texas. As the noon hour approached and the workers were preparing to eat their lunch, four heavily armed men rode up. These strangers directed the work crew to remove the spikes from the rails. No threats were needed as the riders' ready hands on their guns aptly induced the crew to follow their orders. After the spikes had been pulled, the rails were spread to prevent passage of the westbound train that was due to arrive on the scene within a few minutes.

The foreman of the work crew was then sent down the track with a flag to signal the approaching train to stop, that the track ahead was impassable. The four bandits followed the flagman on their horses as he hurried to reach a point that would provide ample distance for the oncoming train to stop before reaching the dismantled rails.

Within a few minutes, passenger train No. 3 came to a halt at the selected site, and the four unmasked men continued with the next step of their planned robbery. They advised the passengers that "you'uns needn't be skeert, it's money we-ere after." Only a few threatening shots were required to convince the train crew and passengers that the hijackers would not tolerate any resistance or even any great display of curiosity.

Two of the robbers took the foreman of the section crew with them into the express car. The other two guarded the train crew and kept an eye on the trailing line of passenger cars. When anyone tried to dismount from one of the cars or even stick his head out of a window, a shot whizzed by, which quickly persuaded him and the rest of the passengers to stay inside. The two road agents in the express car readily gained entry into the small safe and removed its contents, estimated to be ten thousand dollars.

The messenger, Guy Marshall, a long-time employee of the T&P, did not have the combination to the big safe containing the payroll of the Texas and Pacific Coal Company. The payroll safe was being shipped to the company's office at Thurber, the train's next stop after Gordon. Accepting the messenger's statement that he could not open the big safe, the robbers tried to force it open with a pickax.

The train crew, passengers, and section workers were quite passive while the hijackers continued their efforts to carry out their mission. The robbers worked diligently, swinging the pickax at the lock, but the safe withstood their repeating thrusts. After nearly thirty minutes of strenuous exertion, they determined that the safe would not yield. The payroll, estimated as high as sixty thousand dollars, remained intact in the big, battered safe.

With indications of dejection the hijackers then ordered the engineer to move the train some distance back down the track. As the train started moving backward, the road agents rode to the section crew and told them that they could go to work repairing the disabled track. After a short discussion among themselves, the robbers rode into a nearby thicket of bushes and were lost from sight.

The T&P Coal Company had received a tip several days earlier that a robbery of the payroll was being planned. The officers of the firm had considered that the attempt would be made after the safe was received at Thurber, not while en route. The coal company had stationed several armed men in and around its office to prevent the anticipated robbery. Upon receiving word that the train had been attacked, and informed that the payroll was secure, the company dispatched this standby force of men to the scene of the crime, nine miles east of Thurber.[1]

No one had been physically harmed by the hijackers. Even though the robbers had not covered their faces, and had been perplexed by the impregnability of the big safe, they remained calm and business-like. Three of the robbers were described as being of medium height and weight, the other one was noted "as small and wore very small high-heeled boots." They were well dressed and wore gold rings, chains, and watches. After entering the thicket, they first rode south to where they had some horses hidden, then reversed and headed north. One waved his hat as they passed a farmhouse not far from the robbery site. They were riding fine, well-shod horses, one black and three bays. The robbers were later reported to have passed near Coalville.

Within two hours of the robbery, posses from Gordon and Thurber were in pursuit of the outlaws. Captain Owens of the Texas Rangers and Palo Pinto County sheriff Maddox both reached the site of the crime by mid-afternoon. During the night, Texas Ranger captain Bill McDonald, with six of his men and their horses from Amarillo, arrived at Gordon. Captain McDonald and his Rangers were experienced manhunters and were familiar with the hilly terrain of Palo Pinto County. They were expected to locate and bring in the robbers in short order.

The following day Deputy U.S. Marshal S.N. "Sam" Farmer and Parker County sheriff Cleveland arrived at Gordon to help track down the holdup men. Rewards for the arrest and conviction of the guilty parties were being established as more lawmen arrived for the manhunt. The estimated amount of money obtained by the robbers from the smaller safe was revised upward to fifteen thousand dollars. The T&P officials at Thurber could not open the damaged safe. They directed that the safe, still holding the coal company payroll, be delivered to Fort Worth to be opened.[2]

There were no reports of arrest, and as the days passed it appeared that the robbers had made good their escape. One newspaper article noted that an eastbound train had been robbed at the same location a few years earlier.[3]

The Checotah Hardware Company, Checotah, Indian Territory. A prominent business in the Creek Nation. (Courtesy of the Checotah Preservation Society.)

CHAPTER 2

Death of a Deputy
in the Creek Nation

During the first few days following the October 1894 train robbery, several posses combed the hills for miles around Gordon, Texas. The only sightings of the four road agents had been immediately following the robbery. Not finding any new leads, many of the pursuers soon dropped from the manhunt.

Deputy U.S. Marshal Sam Farmer, of the Northern District of Texas, stayed on their trail. He followed the robbers out of Texas, through the Chickasaw Nation, and into Oklahoma Territory, where he lost track of them. The deputy marshal did learn that the suspects had been around Cloud Chief, O.T. (Oklahoma Territory) and, while there, had gotten on very familiar terms with an old Indian. The officer was advised that just before they left that locale the aged Indian mysteriously disappeared. The general opinion was that he had been murdered so he could tell no tales.

Sam Farmer learned that after leaving Washita County the outlaws had passed through the Chickasaw Nation again, but had vanished from that area shortly before he could locate them. Four months after the robbery, the trail led him to the Creek Nation. Deputy Farmer and a fellow officer, J.M. Britton, used aliases when they checked into the Adams Hotel at Muskogee in mid-February of 1895.

The officers began traveling throughout the Creek Nation

searching for the suspects. They located three of the wanted men living in the Checotah/Eufaula area. Farmer wired Deputy U.S. Marshal Lit Williams of Texas to join him and Britton at Checotah.[1]

In preparing for a raid on the suspects' homes to arrest them, Sam Farmer telegraphed U.S. Marshal Rogers at Muskogee and requested that he send a posse. Marshal Rogers returned word that only one officer was available. Deputy Jim Nakedhead, a Cherokee, who was also a member of the Indian Police Lighthorsemen, was sent from the Muskogee marshal's office. From the Checotah area, the Texas officers obtained the services of Deputy Marshal John McCowen, Deputy Sheriff R.N. McClain, Ike Hosey, Lee and Sid Palmer, and a guide.[2]

A few days later, Sam Farmer reported his version of the nine-man expedition in the following account:

> The posse arrived at the house of the Ben Hughes party, ten miles southwest of Checotah, just before daybreak, February 27, 1895. The house was a double-log structure in a bottom, near Deep Fork creek, with a growth of oak around it. We planned to approach the house from two sides, surprise and arrest the occupants. The plan was foiled by two shepherd dogs rushing upon the posse and viciously barking, which alarmed the inmates. Hughes' wife came out and hissed the dogs upon us. A man named Kittrell ran out of the house, then ran back in, when he saw us.
>
> Ben Hughes and a man called Anderson whose real name is Silvers, came rushing down upon us, shooting at every jump. Anderson rushed past us as he fired, and ran into a cotton field, with a volley of our shots following him. As Nakedhead turned to fire at Anderson, Ben Hughes jumped behind a big log and shot the Indian. The ball hit Nakedhead in the right side of the head and passed clear through, he fell flat on his face and expired. Hughes then shot twice at me, while I stood behind a small tree. As he prepared for the third shot, Lit Williams fired at him, striking him in the right shoulder, and he dropped his Winchester. I called on Hughes to surrender. He laid his six-shooter down, and held up his one good hand.[3]

Several years later, Ben Hughes related his version of the gun-fight in the following account:

> "A little before daylight, one morning a posse of federal deputies operating out of the Fort Smith federal court of Judge Parker rode to our home, on the Deep Fork. The possemen dismounted and tied their horses in the woods, near the house and proceeded afoot. As they neared our cabin, my dog barked so violently that we were awakened. My wife thought the dog had bayed the varmint that had been getting her chickens. She ran out the front door and into the yard. I was on the dodge at the time, and although I was satisfied that officers did not know I was in the territory, I took no chances. I grabbed my rifle and a shot sack of cartridges and ran out the back door, into a field near the house.
>
> "The officers without announcing who they were or making any other statement, shot and killed my dog. They fired in the direction of my wife, probably to scare her back into the house. The crash of their rifles had hardly died out, when I fired, breaking Nakedhead's neck. When I fired the officers jumped for shelter behind trees in the yard. I kept my rifle so hot that they couldn't do much, except stick their gun barrels from around the trees, against which they were bellying-up to, as tight as lizards.
>
> 'We must have exchanged two hundred shots. I had the advantage of having them in front of my log, and I barked the trees with bullets every time I saw an elbow, foot or anything else to shoot at. It was now good daylight. One of the men called out, 'we are deputy marshals.' I answered, 'I would have been mighty glad to have heard you say that, an hour or so ago. If you had told me you were deputies when you came up, there would not have been any shooting.'"[4]

The newspaper report went on to say that Mrs. Hughes heard the talking between her husband and the deputies, and thought that her husband was calling for more cartridges. She filled her apron from the reserve supply, kept in the cabin, and ran out the back door. She was captured by the deputies and Hughes surrendered.

Ben's account never mentioned that he had been wounded in the gunfight.

Three of the posse returned to Checotah with the body of Jim Nakedhead, and with Hughes as their prisoner. Later in the day they took Hughes to Muskogee, where he was put in jail. Nakedhead's body was delivered to his family at Tahlequah for burial. From the Hughes place near Brush Hill, the other posse members went to the home of Sam Baker, another of the suspected train robbers who lived about five miles east of Hughes.

Sam Baker (whom the Texas officers then called "Harve Carter") was arrested without incident and taken to Checotah. Later in the day, the third suspect, Shirley Smith (also known by several other names) surrendered to the officers at Checotah.

The following day, Deputy U.S. Marshal Bob Gentry accompanied the remainder of the posse as they delivered Baker and Smith to Muskogee. Gentry had a writ for the prisoners, issued by Marshal Crump of Fort Smith, for the killing of Deputy Nakedhead. The Texas officers objected to giving up the prisoners, claiming they had first rights and should be allowed to hold the "wanted men."[5]

One newspaper account of the October 19, 1894, Texas train robbery mentioned that an eastbound train had been robbed at the same location, the foot of Clayton Mountain, a few years earlier. There was no date cited for the previous robbery, nor was there any indication whether the hijackers had been caught or had escaped. No names were listed of those involved with the previous robbery, nor was anyone named as a suspect of the recent holdup.

Immediately after the arrest of Ben Hughes, one newspaper provided additional information about him and the earlier train robbery near Clayton Mountain: "Hughes is as desperate a character as Texas has produced in recent years." Then, after telling of the recent train robbery, the report continued: "He was tried about five years ago, for train robbery, committed at the same place. Hughes was sentenced to ninety-nine years in the penitentiary, at that time, but got a new hearing and was acquitted."[6]

CHAPTER 3

The Elusive Ben Hughes

After being lodged in the Muskogee jail, Ben Hughes faced charges for both the murder of Deputy Marshal Jim Nakedhead, committed in the Creek Nation, and the 1894 Texas train robbery. There were numerous telegrams sent to and from U.S. Marshal Crump in the matter of holding Hughes for the Fort Smith court, on the murder charge, before permitting the Texas officials to return him to that state. The Texas officers insisted that they had prior claim and that they should be allowed to hold him, at least until they were confirmed to collect the reward. It is not clear what agreement had been reached when U.S. Marshal Rogers released Hughes from the Muskogee jail to be transferred to Texas, in lieu of first being taken to Fort Smith for the murder of Deputy Marshal Nakedhead.[1]

On March 2, 1895, Ben Hughes, Shirley Smith, and Sam Baker (the man the Texas officers called "Harve Carter") were transported by train to Fort Worth as prisoners of Deputy Marshal Sam Farmer and three other officers. Farmer had once been chief of police in Fort Worth. A large crowd had gathered at the train station that afternoon, to greet the locally popular lawman, and to peer at the suspects of the recent train robbery.

Deputy Farmer told a reporter that he had strong evidence against Hughes and Carter, and that he was sure they were the right men. He acknowledged that he did not have as good a case against Smith as he had against the other two. One of Hughes' arms was in a sling, the other was handcuffed to Carter, and he and Carter were more talkative than was Smith. The reporter described the two as being "about forty years old, with appearances that indicate that they are men with plenty of nerve."

The reporter continued his article by stating: "Hughes and Carter have a good deal of the typical border man about them. Smith more nearly resembles a small farmer. The prisoners had little to say about the robbery, each deny that they were involved in it. They claim to be hard working farmers engaged in raising cotton in the Indian Territory. Ben Hughes' wife, who accompanied him is a young looking woman, and not bad looking. She is said to be as nervy as the bold bandits' brides are pictured in romance. It is said that she frequently wore men's apparel with a revolver buckled to her side and rode forth, man fashion on excursions with her husband and his comrades."[2]

When the eastbound train arrived at Fort Worth that evening, the officers escorted their three prisoners aboard for the final leg of their trip. They were taken to Dallas to be tried for the October 19, 1894, train robbery in Palo Pinto County. There was some speculation that Ben's wife may have been one of the four train robbers. Some thought she may have been the one described as "small, and wore very small high-heeled boots." Even if she had not been directly involved in the robbery, the officers surmised that she might be carrying some of the stolen money. Mrs. Hughes remained in Fort Worth when her husband and the other two suspects were taken to Dallas.

The following day, Texas Ranger W.J.L. Sullivan was assigned the task of searching Mrs. Hughes to determine if she had any of the money on her person. Ranger Sullivan later wrote of that experience: "I carried Ben Hughes' wife from the Union depot in Fort Worth to the Windsor Hotel with instructions to make a thorough search for money. Mrs. Windsor, the proprietress of the hotel, assisted me in making the search on Mrs. Hughes' person for the money which we thought her husband had gotten turned over to her. I got Mrs. Windsor to help me in searching the woman, because I felt a delicacy in making the search on the person of a lady, even if I was searching for stolen money. I only found about twelve or fifteen dollars on her, and she said that was her own money, so I let her keep it. She looked to be about twenty-five years of age."[3] Mrs. Hughes left Fort Worth that evening on the train for Palo Pinto County.

No documentation to provide date, details, or dispositions of the trial or trials of the three suspects at Dallas has been located. It may be assumed that the charges were dropped or that the suspects were found not guilty, because Sam Baker was soon back home in the Creek Nation. After disposition of the case against him in Texas, Ben Hughes was delivered to the jail at Fort Smith. There he was indicted on June 27, 1895, for the murder of Deputy Nakedhead.

Ben's brother, Jim, was also a suspect in the 1894 train robbery. Jim was arrested or gave himself up shortly after Ben was caught. Years later, a reporter wrote of their cases: "They were tried separately for the train robbery, Ben in Dallas, and Jim in Fort Worth, and each beat his case."[4]

Ben Hughes' confinement in the Fort Smith Federal jail for the murder of Deputy Nakedhead was not the first time that he had been locked up in that facility. He had been charged with stealing four horses from a James Huffman in the Choctaw Nation ten years earlier, back on October 6, 1885. He was arrested for the crime and was indicted in November 1886. There were some unaccounted for delays in handling the case, because eighteen months later, Ben was still in the Fort Smith jail, or he had been returned to it, to await trial for "larceny of the horses." His father, James S. Hughes Sr., and a J.D. Warren posted a five-hundred-dollar bond on March 28, 1888, at the district court in Graham, Texas, for Ben's release until the first Monday of May.

Ben failed to appear for his trial in Fort Smith, which had been scheduled on the May 1888 docket. The U.S. marshal of the Western District of Arkansas was directed on June 8, 1889, to bring in Hughes for the August 1889 term of court. The warrant was later returned, marked "not served." Another warrant dated February 27, 1890, was issued to the U.S. marshal to have Ben Hughes in court for the term beginning May 5, 1890. That warrant was returned, marked "unexecuted, June 18, 1893." When and how this larceny case against Ben Hughes, which had been pending for eight years, was disposed of is not presently known. It must have been either resolved in some manner satisfactory to the court or lost in the records, because when Ben was charged two years later (in 1895) at Fort Smith for the murder of Deputy Nakedhead, there was no indication that a case of stealing horses was yet pending against him.[5]

The "larceny of horses" had occurred in 1885. Ben had been indicted of the charge in 1886, and the case had not yet been settled in 1893. The previous Texas train robbery had occurred in 1887, for which he had been tried about five years prior to the 1894 train robbery. At Ben's first trial for the 1887 train robbery, he had been convicted and sentenced to ninety-nine years. Due to a technicality Ben was granted a new trial and was then acquitted of the charge. These two cases overlapped.

The sequence of events during this turbulent period of Ben Hughes' life cannot currently be clarified. The series of articles written in 1932 did not mention the charge against Ben for stealing horses and reported only one charge of train robbery. The article stated that "following the [train] robbery, and before their arrest on the charge, the brothers were missing several years." The author was obviously referring to the span of time after the first train robbery (1887) until they were brought in to answer for the second train robbery, in February 1895.

During Ben's confinement in the Fort Smith jail, awaiting trial for the murder of Deputy Nakedhead, his cell mate was James Casharego (AKA "George Wilson"). Casharego was being held for the murder of his traveling companion, Z.W. Thatch, near Keokuk Falls, in northeastern Pottawatomie County.

While Ben was sharing a cell with Casharego in the Fort

Smith lockup, his brother Jim became acquainted with Al Jennings. Al had been Canadian County attorney at El Reno, O.T., but after his defeat for re-election in 1894, he moved to Woodward, O.T. Al joined his brothers John and Ed in their law practice at Woodward. Their father, J.D.F. Jennings, was probate judge of Woodward County at that time. During a trial, one of the Jennings brothers got into a verbal conflict with Temple Houston, another Woodward attorney. Tempers flared, names were called, and threats were made. Court was adjourned to allow the issue to subside.

That evening, October 8, 1895, Temple Houston and his friend John "Jack" Love, a former Woodward County sheriff, were gambling in the Cabinet Saloon at Woodward when John and Ed Jennings entered. A few minutes later, the four men were in a gunfight. Ed Jennings was killed, and John was severely wounded. Neither Houston nor Love was hit. They immediately surrendered to the sheriff and were charged with the murder of Ed Jennings. None of the Jennings family was present at the resulting trial. Houston and Love claimed self-defense, and the jury concluded that they were "not guilty." One witness reported that he believed that Ed was actually killed by wild shots fired by his brother John.[6]

Al later claimed that after his brother Ed was killed, he went gunning for Houston and, in so doing, slipped into the "outlaw world." He had given up practicing law and was beginning to "ride the outlaw trail" when he and Jim Hughes met. Jim prevailed upon Al to go to Fort Smith and assist in Ben's defense. Jennings did go and aid Ben's attorney of record to prepare for the trial, but did not give his right name. In payment for his service, Ben gave Al a map that was claimed to show the location of where seven thousand dollars was buried. The map had been given to Ben by his cell mate, Casharego, who was hanged on July 30, 1896, the last man executed while Isaac Parker served as the judge of the Western District of Arkansas.

At Ben's trial, fellow officers of the deceased Deputy Nakedhead testified that when they went to Ben Hughes' cabin, they knew that he was there. They stated that they were after him specifically for the Texas train robbery, and they did not have time or the opportunity to obtain the official warrants for their mission. The presentation of Ben's defense was well received by the court. Judge Parker instructed the jury that "the defendant had a right to resist such an attack by the officers, who had no warrant for his arrest or their invasion of his home." The jury found Ben Hughes not guilty of the murder of Deputy Nakedhead.[7]

Later, Jennings told Hughes that he had found the flat rock identified on the Casharego map that was represented to mark the spot of the supposed buried treasure. With great anticipation, Al and his cohorts started digging to recover the hidden money. Their efforts were interrupted by an oncoming posse. The Jennings gang got away, and Al never learned if any loot was actually buried there, or if it became the posse's trove.[8]

CHAPTER 4

Sam Baker, an Ally of the Law and the Lawless

Columbus Winfield "Sam" Baker was born on January 24, 1859, near Frankfort, a town in remote northwest Alabama. Little is known of Sam's early life. He married a Francis Brooks in 1879. The Brooks family was then deeply involved in a vendetta which had resulted from the murder of Willis Brooks, the father of Francis and her several brothers. Sam's marriage brought him into the midst of this feud, which had been ongoing since the father of his bride had been killed fifteen years earlier. Baker's guns were a welcome addition to the Brooks clan in their quest to avenge themselves against the men they held responsible for the murder of Willis Brooks.

Five years after Sam had married into the Brooks family, each of the seven men the family held accountable for the murder of their patriarch had paid with his life. By the time their goal was finally realized, Sam Baker and two of his brothers-in-law, Willis Jr. and Henry, were the only surviving participants of the Brooks clan. Their feuding had put them at odds with most of their independent-minded neighbors, and in 1884 they decided to leave Alabama. They settled in Cooke County, in the Cross Timbers area of Texas, and remained there for about six years.

Baker then moved his family to Collins (the name was later changed to Collinsville) in the Cherokee Nation. In 1894,

31

Baker moved his family again — this time to the Creek Nation, near a settlement known as Bond's Switch (it was later named Irby, then still later renamed Onapa) between Eufaula and Checotah. That same year his brother-in-law, Willis Brooks, moved his family into the Dogtown area, west of Eufaula.[1]

After Sam Baker was released from the train robbery charge in Texas, he returned to his home in the Creek Nation. He began to associate with the Jennings brothers, Al and Frank, as they delved deeper into outlawry. Richard "Little Dick" West and Charles (AKA "Dan") "Dynamite Dick" Clifton, former members of the old Doolin gang, had taken up with the Jennings brothers. Sam Baker and Willis Brooks had befriended Little Dick West back when he was a waif in Texas and they were living in Cooke County.

One of the Jennings gang's failed robberies was of a Missouri, Kansas and Texas (MK&T) train, which was attempted near Baker's home. The Jennings gang found a stack of railroad ties at the selected site, which they piled on the rails, then set them afire. The outlaws thought that upon seeing the burning hazard, the engineer would apply the brakes and stop the train. The engineer, however, realized the probable purpose of the obstacle, and instead of slowing, he opened the throttle. The bewildered would-be robbers stood slacked-jawed and dumbstruck as they watched the speeding train tear through the blazing barricade, bounding flaming ties in all directions.

After this attempted train robbery, Deputy U.S. Marshal Bud Ledbetter of Muskogee became convinced that Sam Baker was involved with the Jennings gang. Knowing something of Baker's shady past and suspicious of his current behavior, Ledbetter approached him on the matter and solicited his support to bring in the Jennings boys. Baker and his brother-in-law Willis Brooks agreed to help the deputy in his cause. To provide a link between the popular Muskogee lawman and the two newly recruited informers, Bob Gentry was selected as a go-between to pass information. Gentry lived in Checotah and had previously served as a deputy U.S. marshal.

Columbus Winfield "Sam" Baker. Taken in the 1880s in Alabama. (Courtesy of Edward Herring, Mt. Hope, Alabama.)

Little Dick West and Dynamite Dick Clifton had ridden with the Jennings gang in their early robbery attempts but had quit in disgust as the gang's failures continued. West and Clifton left Al and his boys and went "on their own." There was more loyalty between them and Baker and Brooks than any of the four felt for Al Jennings.

Ledbetter's plan of using Baker and Brooks soon paid off. While pretending to help the Jennings boys get out of the country, Baker delivered them to a creek crossing near his home, where a posse lay in wait. As the team pulled their wagon up the bank of the creek, Deputy Marshal Ledbetter halted the party. He arrested Al and Frank Jennings and another member of their gang on December 6, 1897, without a fight.

After Little Dick West and Dynamite Dick Clifton left the Jennings gang, they continued to be frequent visitors at the homes of Sam Baker, and of Willis Brooks, who lived about thirty-five miles southwest of Baker. Little Dick spent a great deal of his time with a Creek Indian woman who lived near Watsonville, only five miles north of the Brooks place. Dynamite Dick had friends a few miles northwest of Baker's home.

West and Clifton circulated freely throughout the area south and west of Checotah. Two deputy U.S. marshals, George Lawson and "Hess" Bussy, became aware of one of the places that Dynamite Dick often stayed, some ten miles west of Checotah. During the day of November 7, 1897, the lawmen watched and waited for him. Upon his arrival, rifle shots echoed through the hills. One of the first shots broke Clifton's arm, but he was "game" and fought to the end. The officers delivered his body to Checotah. His burial site is not currently known. Another posse of deputy marshals located Little Dick West near Guthrie on April 8, 1898. West also "put-up a fight," but he too was killed.[2] Little Dick was buried in the Summit View Cemetery, Guthrie, O.T. His tombstone incorrectly shows that he was killed on April 13, which was the date of his burial.

Bob Gentry, who had been Baker's contact in Sam's betrayal of the Jennings gang, was the son of a prominent family and

Deputy U.S. Marshal Bud Ledbetter. (From the author's collection.)

operated a profitable business in Checotah. Baker had been
suspected of various crimes and was known to have associated
with numerous outlaws. Later, he became an officer of the law.
In Baker's new role as a deputy city marshal of Checotah, trouble evolved between him and Gentry.[3]

The animosity that developed between the two former con-
federates culminated in the death of Gentry on November 9,
1900. One newspaper reported: "Bob Gentry was drinking, had
a Winchester and was after Deputy City Marshal Sam Baker, on
the streets of Checotah, with a view of shooting him. Baker was
warned by friends and avoided Gentry. Baker was passing the
George Hotel and Gentry stepped from a room near the post
office and knelt down to shoot. Baker leveled his Winchester
and fired, the ball striking Gentry in the abdomen and passing
around and shattering the spinal column. Baker's rifle choked
as he attempted to throw another cartridge into the barrel,
whereupon the marshal drew his pistol and shot Bob in the
breast, the ball passing out through the arm. Gentry died a few
minutes later. Sam Baker went to Muskogee and gave himself
up. He was given a preliminary hearing before Commissioner
Sanson. The testimony showed that Baker had acted in self
defense and he was released."[4]

W.F. (Frank) Jones was a deputy U.S. marshal assigned to
Checotah. Several years later he recorded the following experience with Sam Baker: "Jones found him drunk one day in
Checotah, told him he had better go home. Jones was standing
in front of the Russell Drug Store. Baker went up the street to
Freeman's restaurant, got his gun (he had been courting old
man Freeman's daughter) came to where Jones was and drew
his gun on him, Jones beat him to the draw, shot him through,
just above the heart, and paralyzed him. Baker asked to be
taken to the Freeman restaurant where he lay unconscious for
two days." Baker later recovered and accepted all of the blame
for the trouble.[5]

A newspaper item about this incident reports that it occurred
on August 23, 1902, and that two shots were fired, both by Jones.

His pistol was deflected by Baker's hand, causing his first shot to accidently strike a George D. Howard who was unaware of the trouble and was passing near by. His second shot entered Baker's left breast, passing through his body and out near his shoulder blade. Baker's wound was thought to be fatal. George Howard died a few hours after being hit and was buried the next day. Another bystander was slightly injured in the shooting affair. Jones was taken to Muskogee, bail was raised, and he was released to await a hearing. Later, it was determined that he was not guilty of any wrongdoing.[6]

Sam Baker became involved in yet another feud that had developed between his brother-in-law Willis Brooks and one of Willis' neighbors, Jim McFarland. Baker was not present when that trouble exploded with gunfire, bringing death to three men. That shoot-out occurred about a month after Baker had been shot and seriously wounded by Jones.[7]

Deputy Marshal Frank Jones captured Jim Holbrook and another outlaw near Henryetta on September 24, 1902. Holbrook was wanted for numerous crimes in the Territories. He had been a member of the Bert Casey gang, and a confederate of Sam Baker. Jim was also a supporter of Willis Brooks in his feud with the McFarland clan.[8]

Sam Baker was serving as McIntosh County deputy sheriff when Chitto Harjo (also known as "Wilson Jones"), a leader of the Creek Indians, resisted the Federal government's efforts to assign individual land allotments. Harjo's refusal to cooperate in the dispersal of tribal land brought forth hundreds of other malcontent Indians and Freedmen who rallied around him, anxious to defy the order.

The man known by many as Chitto Harjo, which translated to "Crazy Snake," was usually referred to by that name, and his followers were called "Snake Indians." They set up camp at Hickory Ground (at the western edge of McIntosh County, about ten miles east of Henryetta), and it became recognized as their home. Their revolt, often referred to as the "Crazy Snake Rebellion," was the last major uprising in Indian Territory. Deputy

Marshal Frank Jones of Checotah led several posses to the Hickory Ground to make arrests and control the Snakes.

Harjo and his followers seized fellow Creeks who had accepted their assigned land allotments, then whipped them in public. Some were reported to have been killed in these floggings. The trouble started in 1902. As the havoc continued, Crazy Snake and some of his followers were convicted and sent to prison for two years. After their release, Harjo and his Snake Indians would frequently surface again, disrupting the peaceful Indians and frightening the white settlers. There had been numerous confrontations between officers of the law and the uprising Indians. In 1909, the Snakes, led by Chitto Harjo, again set up camp at Hickory Ground.

Dock Odom was sheriff of McIntosh County, and his office was at Eufaula, the county seat. Checotah, equal in size to Eufaula, had been trying to gain the county seat. Odom appointed his son Herman as undersheriff, and the son then maintained an office at Checotah. A warrant was issued for the arrest of Crazy Snake, which was sent to the Checotah office. Herman and five deputies went to Chitto Harjo's place (about fifteen miles west of Checotah, near Pierce). As they approached Crazy Snake's home on March 27, 1909, the lawmen encountered a large band of Indians and were fired upon. A gunfight ensued, in which Deputies Herman Odom and Ed Baum were killed. Frank Jones and the other three possemen were held under fire for some time but managed to escape the overpowering force.

Sheriff Odom telephoned Governor Charles Haskell and requested that the state militia be sent to help prevent a general uprising. Sheriff Odom was determined to arrest Crazy Snake, and believed him to be hiding at his home. He took Frank Jones, Sam Baker, and six other deputies with him and on March 29, 1909, they headed for Harjo's home. As they approached, they were shocked to see the house burst into flames. Suddenly the posse was fired upon, and they scurried for cover. Baker ran through the timber toward the house and saw one of the Indians who was shooting. Baker killed him, then spotted another. After a chase the second Indian met the same fate. The first Indian felled by Baker was Charlie Coker. It was thought that Coker had fired the shot that had killed Deputy Baum in the previous gunfight. Baker's second victim was never identified. Crazy Snake was not found.

Colonel Roy Hoffman arrived at Henryetta with one company of militia from Muskogee and another from Chandler. Hoffman marched his troops to Hickory Ground. The Snakes had obviously heard that the army was coming, as the Indians had moved out before the military arrived. Although they had scattered, the National Guard began rounding them up. The military captured eighty-six of the armed Snake Indians. Those captured by the various posses brought the total to about one hundred and fifty, which accounted for most of Chitto Harjo's followers who were active in the latter stages of the Crazy Snake Rebellion. The state militia received orders to return to their home bases and departed from Henryetta on April 2, 1909.[9]

There were many stories told after the disappearance of Crazy Snake. Each was supposed to reveal the real truth of his demise. One such story related that Deputy Marshal Frank Jones and Deputy Sheriff Sam Baker found Harjo with four of his guards. The two lawmen were reported to have killed them all and thrown their bodies in the river. A more plausible account related that the human bones found in Harjo's burnt-out house were those of Crazy Snake, that Harjo had been killed in the March 27 attack on his house, and that his body was in the home when the sheriff's posse approached two days later. Harjo's house had been burned to disfigure his body so that the officers could not identify him and learn that Crazy Snake had succumbed to their bullets.

The most popular account is attributed to Fred Barde, a newspaper reporter who covered the final days of the rebellion. He returned to the area four years later and conducted his personal investigation. He reported that Crazy Snake had been hit by a bullet during the same gunfight in which Deputies Odom and

Baum had been killed. His guards left that night taking the wounded Harjo, traveling southeast over the mountains.

Ultimately, they reached the remote home of Harjo's friend Daniel Bob in McCurtain County. Barde obtained a statement from Daniel Bob acknowledging that Harjo had arrived at his farm and had remained with him until Crazy Snake's death on April 11, 1911. Some fifty years later the Oklahoma Historical Society placed a plaque in the yard of the old Daniel Bob farm (about five miles southwest of Smithville) in commemoration of Crazy Snake.[10]

Sam Baker's entire adult life had been filled with violence. It was reported that he had killed one or more men in the feud before leaving Alabama. He had shot and killed one man and had himself been seriously wounded in another gunfight on the streets of Checotah. He had killed two Indians during the Crazy Snake Rebellion. Sam was considered to be a "fightin' man."

C.P. Torrans (some records have the name as Torrence) and his son W.P. "Will" Torrans operated a store in Checotah, to which Baker was in debt for a purchase. They thought that he was trying to ignore them and forego his payment. Baker, with his "rough and ready" attitude, paid but little attention to the younger Torrans when Will complained to him about his unpaid bill. After Will gained no satisfaction, the father and son decided that more drastic action might be required to settle the matter.

About a week after Will Torrans had reminded Baker of his debt, and there was still no acknowledgement from him, the merchants took action. As Baker walked down a crowded street in Checotah on October 7, 1911, he passed in front of the Torrans' store. C.P. and Will approached him. Immediately after confronting Baker, the father and son each fired a shot. One shot went wild, but the other passed through Baker, and he died about three hours later. Sam was buried in the Checotah Cemetery alongside his wife Francis, who had died twelve years previously. The Torrans were held in the Eufaula jail and charged with Baker's murder.[11]

The Torrans requested to be released on bail. Their first request was refused, but then Judge Henry M. Furman of the appeals court in Oklahoma City overruled that denial. Bonds in the amount of five thousand dollars for Will and twenty-five hundred dollars for C.P. were raised with the First National Bank of Muskogee. The father and son merchants were released on October 24, 1911, to await their trial for the murder of Sam Baker.[12]

A few days later Judge Furman issued a clarification of his ruling in the Torrans case which included this statement: "A son has the right to shoot his father's assailants in defense of the father. There is no law which requires a son to act the contemptible coward, base counterfeit upon true manhood's coin, when he sees his father in imminent danger of receiving serious bodily injury, but he may act in his defense instantly, with the most deadly and effective weapons at his command, provided only that he acts in good faith and upon reasonable apprehension of danger. To deny such right would be revolting to justice and in utter disregard to the most sacred ties of human nature."[13]

McIntosh County court records for felony cases of that period are not currently available. Disposition of the court case against the Torrans for the murder of Sam Baker is not known.[14]

CHAPTER 5

Vengeance to the Death

Willis Brooks Jr. was born on April 3, 1854, to Willis and Sarah Jane Brooks who lived in Lawrence County, Alabama. Lawrence and the adjoining Winston County were situated in the heart of the "hill country" of northwestern Alabama. The land was not suitable for farming and raising cotton. The economic conditions and social life of the region differed greatly from the rest of the state.

As the Civil War approached, these differences became more acute. When Alabama seceded from the Union and joined the Confederacy, an effort was made in Winston County to secede from Alabama and remain with the Union. The majority of residents were called "Tories" and had no desire to help the South protect and maintain its ways and means of living which were vastly unlike those of the hill folks of northwestern Alabama. Most of those who lived in the area considered the conflict between the North and the South to be "a rich man's war and a poor man's fight." The main interest of most families in the hill country was not based on loyalty to either side, nor concern over the issues involved, but their passion to practice and preserve their mountaineer ways.

When the conflict between the North and the South escalated to armed encounters, many of the young men in the area moved to the "western frontier" to escape the Civil War. Others of the region went north and joined the Union army, while some stayed at home and resisted Confederate conscription.

In the midst of this hotbed of Tories lived Willis and Sarah Jane Brooks with their eight children. Their offspring had inherited a fraction of Indian blood from their mixed-blood Cherokee mother, and from each parent the rudiments necessary to develop a strong character. The Brooks family sided with the South. They had nothing in common with the plantation owners, and very little kinship with the small farmers of the South, but for some reason they choose to oppose their neighbors and support the Rebel cause. Willis Sr. tried to join the Confederate army, but was rejected because he was fifty-five years old. He did travel with and assist a Confederate cavalry troop for several months, working as a saddle maker.

When Willis returned home in 1863, from his tenure of "aiding the cause," he learned that while he was away a local Tory leader had been annoying his wife. Within a few days, he located the man and killed him. A short time later, seven men rode to the Brooks home, called Willis out, and gunned him down.

From that time forward, Widow Brooks (some twenty years younger than her deceased husband) stressed to her sons that all seven of the men must pay with their lives for the murder of their father. Sarah Jane had seen the men and vouched that she knew their identity. The sons vowed to carry out their mother's wishes. A few days after Willis was buried, his eldest son John was killed while working in a field near the Brooks home.

Most of the men Sarah Jane named as responsible for the murder of Willis Brooks moved north during the latter part of the Civil War. As the Brooks boys matured, they left Alabama and made their way west, but Sarah Jane and the smaller children remained in the hill country. When any of the seven guilty men returned to their old stomping grounds, she would send word to her sons. One or more of her boys would return home, execute the man, and leave the country again, with hardly anyone knowing that they had been back to Alabama. One of the sons disappeared in Indian Territory while on a cattle drive.

When Sam Baker married into the Brooks family, he immediately became one of their "top guns." By late 1883, the Brooks clan had disposed of the last of the seven slayers of their father, but they continued to harass some of their neighbors. Lawrence County sheriff Alex Heflin was fed up with the Brooks boys' continuous "hell-raising."

Heflin deputized some of their neighbors, and in April 1884 a gun battle ensued between these opposing forces in which one deputy was killed and two were wounded. Gaines Brooks was also killed in this gunfight, and bullets shattered the leg of Henry, the youngest of the Brooks boys. To escape the numerous charges pending against them, and the wrath of their neighbors, the Brooks clan decided that it was time to leave Alabama.

They made their way to Cherokee (a small town in the extreme northwestern corner of the state) where, with their families, Willis Brooks Jr., Sam Baker, and the wounded Henry boarded a westbound train. For the next six years they lived in Cooke County, Texas, then Willis moved to Grady, a small settlement just north of the Red River in the Chickasaw Nation. In 1894 Brooks moved his family again, this time to the Creek Nation, about twenty-five miles west of Eufaula.

In this locale, then known as the Dogtown area, Willis prospered. He soon had nearly a hundred horses, and was raising some crops. He also had six enterprising headstrong sons: Thomas, Clifton, John, Earl, Marion, and Willis III. Four miles north of Brooks' place (near Watsonville) lived Jim McFarland, a man with a bad reputation who frequently got himself into trouble with the law. He was the leader of the McFarland clan. Jim had two brothers, Sam and Joe, and a brother-in-law, "Sandy" Watson, who supported him in his devilment.

For about two years the McFarlands and the Brookses were on friendly terms. Trouble began to brew between the two families when Tom, the oldest of the Brooks boys, was killed on April 24, 1896. Tom was attempting to rob a former Texas Ranger who lived in the community. It had been locally rumored for years that the old Ranger had a cache of money.

Willis Brooks believed that Jim McFarland had prompted his son Tom to rob the old man, then alerted the intended victim of Tom's plan. McFarland claimed that Tom had been running with some young men in the community and that the gang of boys were planning to rob the old man, but that Tom had gotten greedy and tried to pull the job alone. To no one's surprise the old Ranger shot and killed him.

This loss of his oldest son set Willis Brooks and Jim McFarland on a course that developed into a feud between the two families. From that time forward the conflict between the Brookses and the McFarlands grew more challenging and bitter. Alonzo "Lon" Riddle and his father, George (known as "Old Man Riddle"), took up with the McFarlands, after the Riddles and the Brookses had trouble.[1]

Henry Brooks' leg, which had been injured in the gunfight with the sheriff's deputies in Alabama, had been amputated and in due course he had become known as "Peg-leg." Deputy U.S. Marshal Frank Jones arrested Henry Brooks on a charge of stealing horses and delivered him to the Lincoln County jail at Chandler. Henry had a relative living close to Chandler who visited the prisoner and pretended to bring him a treat, some syrup. This so-called syrup was not for Peg-leg's appetite, but was actually an acid that would eat metal. Henry hid the acid in the hollow of his wooden leg and applied it to the bars of his cell at every opportunity. Lincoln County sheriff Bill Tilghman learned of Peg-leg's secretive efforts. Tilghman confiscated Brooks' "syrup," which stopped his attempt to break jail. Peg-leg was convicted on the "larceny of horses" charge and was sentenced to serve two years in prison.[2]

In December 1900, Clifton Brooks was arrested and held in the McIntosh County jail. The local newspaper reported: "Clifford [sic] Brooks, son of Willis Brooks of Eufaula District, was arrested Wednesday by Deputy Grant Johnson, charged with various crimes from burglary to murder. He was confined in the Eufaula jail. Late the same night several armed men went to the jail, frightened away the guard, broke down the door and released the prisoner. His horse was waiting for him at the livery stable near the Catholic church. He rode out the back gate of the stable enclosure and away. Willis Brooks, father of the prisoner, was in Eufaula that night, and several suspicious parties were also here but so far there is no evidence against anyone in the matter of jail breaking." The article continued to comment about how slick and quiet the job was pulled and noted that the authorities were confident that Deputy Johnson would soon have the wanted man behind bars again.[3]

Late in 1901, Jim McFarland became a suspect in a murder case. There was not enough evidence to hold him in jail for the crime, and he was released, but continued to be a suspect. Soon thereafter, McFarland's riderless horse with a blood-soaked saddle came home. It was assumed that Jim had been bushwhacked, and the Brookses were suspected, but his body could not be found. A short time later officials learned that Jim was in Mexico and had staged the facade to cover his escape.[4]

The Fort Smith and Western Railroad was being built between Fort Smith, Arkansas, and Guthrie, Oklahoma Territory. During the summer of 1902, roadway construction approached the Dogtown area. The railroad company wanted another town built along the tracks in the Creek Nation, but tribal ownership of the land encumbered such development.

Morton Rutherford and Jesse Hill obtained the contract with the railroad company to develop a townsite in the desired area. The Rutherfords had been prominent citizens of the Indian Nations for nearly a hundred years. Morton had served as U.S. marshall of the Muskogee District from 1895 to 1897 and was currently a deputy U.S. marshal. Both Rutherford and Hill were attorneys. They were well qualified to cope with the land title problems of opening a town in the Creek Nation. Other problems, not anticipated, soon appeared. The selected site lay ominously between Jim McFarland's place on the north and Willis Brooks' land on the south.

Rutherford and Hill chose to call their new town "Spokogee," a Creek word meaning "Near to God." Lots went on sale on July 1,

1902, for twenty-five dollars each, their location to be determined by lottery. The promoters planned well for the big event with free barbecue and other attractions. Hundreds of people attended, and sales were brisk until the affair was disrupted by a fistfight that broke out between John Brooks and Lon Riddle. Sam Baker started to take it up on behalf of his nephew John, but Rutherford got the drop on Sam with his rifle. The deputy marshal escorted Baker to his wagon, where he sat and "gobbled like an Indian" while the crowd dissipated. The opening day sale had been greatly curtailed by the trouble between the feuding families.

The post office at Watsonville was moved to the new townsite and renamed Spokogee. Those folks who had purchased lots and had started to build soon became uneasy on account of the feud between the Brookses and the McFarlands. When members of either family were in town, there was anxiety that members of the other family would ride in and fill the air with flying bullets.

As Rutherford and Hill tried to boost Spokogee and promote its development, more key members of the feuding families arrived on the scene. Peg-leg Brooks was released from prison in July and moved in with his brother Willis. A few weeks later, Jim McFarland returned from his self-imposed exile in Mexico.[5]

McFarland was still trying to convince the citizenry that he had been ambushed and abducted to Mexico. He presented himself at a Eufaula newspaper office along with the saddle that he was supposedly riding at the time that he claimed he was ambushed and suddenly disappeared from the Creek Nation. After observing the saddle, the editor wrote: "It was reported at that time, that the saddle was shot full of holes and covered with blood. Upon careful examination of the saddle, we found plenty of evidence of blood but only one bullet hole, which barely hit the edge of the seat. Jim had the saddle expressed to him in Mexico, and has used it constantly ever since. The charges pending against him at the time of his departure to Mexico were thrown out of court last week."[6]

The ongoing feud between the Brooks and McFarland families cast a pall upon the struggling young town. Spokogee's promoters, Rutherford and Hill, strived to attract more people and to dispel the effect of the feuding families. Progress was slow and disappointing.

One autumn morning, the McFarlands and Riddles rode into Spokogee. Old Man Riddle went about taking care of their errands. About an hour later, Willis Brooks, accompanied by his sons Clifton ("Cliff") and John, all well armed, rode in and hitched their horses. As they entered the post office, they met Old Man Riddle leaving with his mail. The Brookses began to abuse and threaten him. He responded by stating: "Kill me if you want, I am unarmed and have but one time to die." Whereupon, the Brookses cursed him and brandished their weapons, causing Riddle to flee across the street appealing to Rutherford for protection. Rutherford shouted to Brooks and his boys, "Don't shoot, Willis, I am the United States Marshal here and I command peace." Before the words cleared the marshal's mouth a shot was heard and Old Man Riddle fell on his face, mortally wounded. Then another shot was fired from an unknown quarter and Willis Brooks jumped high into the air then fell head first. Dazed and wounded, he rose to his knees and rapidly fired his weapon. Then, riddled with bullets, he fell onto the street. A fusillade of shots followed, during which Cliff Brooks was killed and his younger brother John was badly shot up.

The feud between the Brookses and the McFarlands, which had simmered and threatened for six years in the Dogtown area, exploded with gunfire on September 22, 1902, on the street in Spokogee, Creek Nation. Three men were killed and one seriously wounded.

After the smoke cleared, Deputy Marshal Rutherford arrested Jim and Joe McFarland and Lon Riddle for the murder of the Brookses. He started to Eufaula with his three prisoners and met Deputy U.S. Marshal Grant Johnson on the road. Rutherford turned his prisoners over to Johnson and returned to Spokogee. The accused parties were jailed at Eufaula. They were given a hearing in the commissioner's court the following day and were charged with murder. Bond was raised, and they were released from jail to await trial.[7]

Willis and his son Cliff were buried beside Thomas, who had been killed by the former Texas Ranger, six years earlier. Their graves are in the Checotah cemetery. John Brooks recovered from the gunshot wounds that he received in the gunfight at Spokogee and lived for many years.

Just as tensions in the area began to ease, the community was shocked again. Less than three weeks after the big gunfight in Spokogee, Jim McFarland was murdered on October 10, 1902. He was shot from ambush while riding with his wife in a buggy, as they approached the river crossing near old Watsonville. The couple was returning to their home from a trip to Weleetka when one shot was fired, by an unknown party. The steel-tipped bullet hit Jim in the back and caused his death within minutes.[8]

Sam Baker and Peg-leg Brooks were immediately suspected of McFarland's murder, but there was no evidence and neither was arrested. The first newpaper account of McFarland's death reported that he and Peg-leg Brooks had killed each other at Weleetka.[9] The incorrect information in that first report about Peg-leg having also been killed has been related in some accounts written about the Brooks family.[10] It has also been incorrectly reported that Peg-leg Brooks left Indian Territory shortly after Willis was killed and returned to Alabama, where he lived the remainder of his life.[11]

The whereabouts of Henry "Peg-leg" Brooks for nearly three years following the big shootout at Spokogee is not presently known. The next confirmed information about him is that he was tried and convicted at Anadarko, in May 1905, for stealing horses in Caddo County. He was sentenced to ten years in prison and was sent to Leavenworth, Kansas, to serve the time.[12]

Information recorded at the time that he entered the prison system, on May 20, 1905, shows that he was: forty-three years old, five feet seven inches tall, weighed 168 pounds, was a native

Street scene in early-day Dustin, Oklahoma. (Courtesy of Edward Herring, Mt. Hope, Alabama.)

of Alabama, had received six months schooling, his mother's name was Jane Johnson (she had remarried), and his occupation was listed as a broom maker (likely a job that he had performed during his previous prison sentence). In January 1909, Peg-leg was transferred from Leavenworth to the new prison facility being constructed at McAlester, Oklahoma. After serving nearly six years of his sentence, Henry Brooks was granted parole on January 10, 1911.[13]

Shortly after being released from the penitentiary at McAlester, Peg-leg Brooks left Oklahoma and returned to northwestern Alabama. He married a young lady and started raising a family. Henry frequently joined the various posses of the sheriff of Lawrence County during World War I. According to local sources, he appeared to be very handy with his rifle and leaned hard on the slackers in the area.

Peg-leg became rather unpopular, especially in the adjoining county of Winston, where the local folks so well remembered the Brooks boys' vendetta following the Civil War. It became rumored that Peg-leg was running a moonshine still, near the county line. A group of Winston County officers were at the site when Brooks approached to refuel his still on Sunday morning, January 11, 1920. The officers claimed that they were not aware that the still's location was across the line in Lawrence County and that, upon seeing the officers, Peg-leg had fired at them. Twelve bullets ended the life of Henry, the last living son of Willis Sr. and Sarah Jane Brooks. His mother was still living at the time that Henry was killed, and it is reported that she calmly commented: "They all died with their boots on, like men." Her simple statement reflected upon the deaths of her husband, five sons, two grandsons, and one son-in-law.[14]

Spokogee survived its troubled infancy and the name was changed in 1904. Five hundred citizens in Hughes County are proud of their hometown, which was first named Spokogee, and has for the last ninety years been known as Dustin.

CHAPTER 6

The Casey Clan

The first census of the newly opened Oklahoma Territory was taken in 1890. The record of that census for County #4 (later named Canadian) shows that George W. (Washington) Casey, was the fifty-nine-year-old head of house, along with his fifty-seven-year-old wife, Justean. Other members of the household were listed as William, son, age 22; James B., son, age 15; Victor M., son, age 12; Essie C., grandaughter, age 10; and William E., grandson, age 8.[1]

The Caseys had lived in the Chickasaw Nation prior to the opening of the "Unassigned Lands." One newspaper reported: "In 1889, George with three sons Dave, Jim and Vic robbed and killed two old men in the Arbuckle Mountains, near where the Caseys then lived. It was also said, that they had robbed and murdered several peddlers in the same vicinity, previous to killing the two old men."[2] At the time that these murders were reported to have occurred, James B. ("Jim") would have been only fourteen years old and Victor ("Vic") a mere eleven.

Canadian County was a part of the Unassigned Lands that had been opened for settlement in the "run of '89," and the elder Casey obtained a homestead on Mustang Creek, near El Reno. Later, when the Cheyenne-Arapaho lands were opened in 1892, the Caseys settled in the Washita River bottoms southwest of Arapaho, in Custer County.

After the family moved to the new homestead, Jim and Vic occasionally returned to their old home area along Mustang Creek, in Canadian County. In May 1894, the two Casey boys became suspects in the murder of the Townsend brothers. The Townsends were bachelors and had been neighbors of the Casey family, when they lived near El Reno. Canadian County deputy sheriff Sam Farris recognized the suspects as they rode into Yukon (ten miles east of El Reno) on May 21, 1894, and tied their horses in front of the Walker Saloon.[3]

As Farris approached to arrest the youths, they each pulled a pistol and fired at the officer. One of their shots hit the lawman in the abdomen. The wounded deputy reeled, but steadied himself, then drew his weapon and fired at the brothers. The shooting continued until both of the boys' guns were empty. Vic and Jim then backed away to reload their Colts, as Farris sent his last cartridge in their direction. Before they could return to the fallen officer, other men from nearby entered the fight and subdued Jim, but Vic escaped. As Vic rode away, one of his wild shots hit an old man by the name of Snyder in the head, causing a wound that was considered likely to prove fatal.[4]

Deputy Farris died that night. Vic was captured a few days later by a posse led by Chris Madsen. He was found hiding in a shelter on the Washita River, near his father's place, in Custer County.[5]

The Casey brothers were transferred from El Reno to the Oklahoma City jail. Jim and Vic Casey, along with two other prisoners, Ed Cox and Charles Lawson, escaped from their Oklahoma City confinement on August 16, 1894. The four inmates cut the steel rivets of the lock on the cell door and removed the brick from the wall of the building. "Tom King" (an alias of Flora Quick Mundis) had previously escaped from the jail cell in the same way. The Casey brothers were later captured, in the area where Vic had been found before. Jim and Vic were returned to the Oklahoma City jail.[6]

In the gunfight at Yukon in which Deputy Farris was fatally wounded, Vic was shot in the foot. His wound was badly infected when he was captured by the Madsen posse. It had not completely healed when he and Jim broke out of jail. After Vic was returned to the Oklahoma City jail, his wound continued to worsen. Blood poisoning set in, and on November 12, 1894, Victor Casey died at the age of sixteen, while a prisoner awaiting trial for the murder of Sam Farris, deputy sheriff of Canadian County.[7]

After Vic's death, while Jim was being held on the same murder charge, the surviving brother became well acquainted with two other inmates, Bill and Bob Christian. The Christian brothers were being held in the Oklahoma City jail awaiting the outcome of their appeal of their conviction for the murder of Will Turner, a Pottawatomie County deputy sheriff.

During their confinement, the Christian brothers obtained some pistols, and reckoned to share them with their fellow lawman slayer. They hid these guns in their cell until an opportune time for the three prisoners to make their escape.

On Sunday evening, June 30, 1895, Bill and Bob Christian with Jim Casey, the three most desperate men in jail, made their break. As the trio fled down the alley, Jim shot and killed Police Chief Milton Jones. A few moments later, Jim Casey was shot and killed by Oklahoma City officer Jackson. Bill and Bob Christian got away and renewed their criminal careers in the Twin Territories. Later, the Christian brothers moved on to Arizona, where each was slain, putting an end to their lives of crime.[8]

Within a few years after Jim Casey was killed in the Oklahoma City jail break, another young Casey, Bert, became a thorn in the side of lawmen. Most of the contemporary newspaper articles about Bert's outlaw career identify him as the brother of the deceased Jim and Vic. These articles also refer to his father as living in the same locales as those in which George W. Casey then lived. The census records of 1890 do not show another son younger than Vic, but they do list a grandson, William. One source states that Bert was the son of Dave, who was an older brother of Jim and Vic.[9]

It may be presumed that Bert was raised by his grandparents,

George and Justean Casey, along with his sister Essie. Since there was a twenty-two-year-old son, William, still at home (1890 census), it is logical that the eight-year-old may have been called by a name other than the typical "Bill," in this case, "Bert." Since he was raised with Jim and Vic, it would be only natural for people to assume that Bert was their younger brother. It is also likely that other than being raised by his grandparents, Bert's youth was typical of other children raised in the Territory. He probably received only limited schooling and encountered the prevailing hardships of the frontier.

The 1900 census of Custer County does not list William E. (grandson Bert) as still being a member of the G.W. Casey household. It does, however, name some other children as living with their aged grandparents, as was the case ten years previously.[10] Soon after the 1900 census was taken, G.W. Casey was appointed guardian of three minor heirs of Frank Casey, deceased.[11]

Undoubtedly, the crisis suffered by the Casey family, when Jim and Vic were charged with murder and then subsequently died at the hands of the law, had a strong impact on the twelve-year-old boy, Bert. These men were not only his uncles but, due to living arrangements, would have seemed like brothers. While they were hiding from the law, near their father's farm, it likely fell Bert's lot to act as courier. This role would have led him to feel that he had been a very important part of their short, turbulent lives. Due to the closeness that Bert must have felt for his uncles, especially for Vic, who was only four years his senior, their sad destiny surely had an enduring influence on his future.

CHAPTER 7

The Hughes Ranch and Bert Casey

James Hughes was born in Missouri, in 1820, one year before that state entered the Union. As a young man he scouted with Kit Carson and Jim Bridger. He was on at least one of John C. Frémont's expeditions to the Far West. James roamed the West until the mid-1850s when he returned to Missouri and married Mary McFarland, who was three years his junior. While they were living in Missouri, their two sons were born: James S. Jr. ("Jim") in 1858, and Benjamin F. ("Ben") in 1860.[1]

The senior Hughes moved his young family to Texas, where he became a prosperous farmer and stockman. He provided well for his family, tilling the Texas soil and raising cattle. When his industrious sons reached maturity, they began to branch out. Railroads were crossing Texas in the mid-1880s, and the boys started contracting some of the preliminary dirt work for the construction crews to lay the rails. It was during this period of Ben's life that he was arrested for stealing horses in Indian Territory. That charge and later, the train robbing charges in Texas against Ben and Jim, kept the brothers "on the dodge" for several years.

The elder Hughes was never accused of being involved with any of his sons' suspected crimes. He was well respected within the community and continued to maintain a good personal reputation, but in 1894 he decided to leave Texas. His search for a

new location took him to the recently settled Cheyenne-Arapaho lands. This area had been opened for homesteading in
the third land run on April 19, 1892, and became a part of Oklahoma Territory. He was attracted to the fertile soil and water
supply that the Washita River provided. Hughes bought the
pending rights to a homestead that fronted on the river southeast of Cloud Chief, then the county seat of "H" County, later
named Washita.[2]

Some of the homesteaders, especially those with large families, found that it was nearly impossible to survive on their mea-
ger resources. With hardly any farm equipment, only a few head
of livestock, and no experience at farming in the new locale—
coupled with the unpredictable weather and poor markets—
these early-day Oklahomans faced hardships that tested the
endurance of the most hardy.

Considering his advanced age, the seventy-five-year-old James
was hale and hearty, except for failing eyesight. The senior
Hughes had assets which he invested wisely in his farm. There
was an ample supply of settlers in the Cloud Chief area who
were hard-pressed for money and were willing to work for a few
dollars. Hughes was an able manager and hired these neighbors
to help him in developing his homestead while his sons were
eluding the law. The land proved worthy of his appraisal, and
within a few years his farm became very productive. When Jim
and Ben got clear of the criminal charges pending against
them, they anxiously joined their father. The father and sons
then began to expand the ranch rapidly.

By 1897, some of the settlers had met the five-year requirement of living on the land and were receiving the patents to
their homesteads. As soon as some of these farmers obtained
the deeds to their one hundred and sixty acres, they gladly sold
out to get some cash and escape the privations of homesteading.
The Hughes brothers were able to purchase several of these
quarter-section tracts.

As the brothers bought more land, they also traded some of
their newly purchased farms for others and joined their holdings with their father's estate. Jim and Ben each built impressive

Drilling a well on Main Street, Cloud Chief, Oklahoma Territory, 1898. (Courtesy of Oklahoma Historical Society.)

homes on their property. As these land deals continued, they brought in more cattle and more farm equipment and hired more "hands" to carry on their ever-enlarging enterprise. During the last years of the nineteenth century, the Hughes brothers obtained a contract to deliver the mail from Weatherford to Cloud Chief and Cordell. This was another operation for the ranch, and still more young men were hired for this project.

Rumors that had filtered in from Texas and Indian Territory, and the fast expansion of their ranch, caused some of their neighbors to become suspicious of their operations. As the neighbors learned more of the Hughes brothers' past, they became doubtful that all was honorable at the ranch. Stories began to circulate that some of the employees and guests at the Hughes place were "men on the scout." It was further speculated that through these shady characters the Hughes brothers were enhancing their prosperity.

Specific names began to be applied to the outlaws who were thought to visit the ranch and partake of the Hughes brothers' hospitality. It was rumored that George "Red Buck" Weightman and George Miller had stayed at the ranch as guests of Jim Hughes, when all three were being sought by the law. There were reports that Al Jennings and his gang camped at the Hughes ranch during their outlaw days. Ben Cravens, a prison escapee and noted outlaw of the time, was thought to frequently "hide-out" at their ranch on the Washita.[3]

Bert Casey was one of the young men who found employment at the Hughes ranch when the brothers obtained the contract "to carry the mail." Bert had left his grandparents' home, twenty-five miles upstream on the Washita, and was hired to drive a mail hack.

Young Casey was much impressed with his forty-year-old bosses, who were "men of means." The Hughes brothers showed a special interest in Bert as they learned more of his family's encounters with lawmen and jails. Casey had a yen and talent to steal horses and he was soon spending most of his time in the pursuit of his calling.

As Bert Casey applied his trade of stealing horses, robbing travelers, and committing other acts of thievery, his adopted home, "the Hughes Ranch on the Washita," grew and prospered. Casey was suspected of many crimes and was "wanted by the law." The Hughes ranch provided him a safe haven. Officers had no picture of him, and he was able to avoid capture while on his forays. Bert's success in his chosen field led him to expand his range. He started engaging in other activities independent of the Hughes ranch.[4]

CHAPTER 8

The Murder of Rufus Choat

By March of 1901, Bert Casey had joined with another young man by the name of Tom Powell. They were operating a saloon known as "The Box" at Young's Crossing on the Canadian River, in the southeast corner of Pottawatomie County. The saloon was a shanty-type structure, built on stilts just north of mid-channel in the meandering river. The purpose of this location was so that whiskey could be sold legally in Oklahoma Territory, yet be as handy as possible for the citizens of the Chickasaw Nation. The Canadian River was the dividing line between the wide-open liquor trade, in Oklahoma Territory, and Prohibition, which was the "law" but not the practice of many who lived in Indian Territory.[1]

Some of its more rugged patrons merely waded the usually shallow water and climbed the short ladder to enter the saloon; most, however, negotiated the wobbly makeshift wooden walkways. Sometimes they combined the two methods; after starting out upon the unstable gangway, they would find themselves in the wading area. This maneuver occurred more frequently when leaving the saloon than it did on approaching the establishment. On at least one occasion during a flood, the structure's supports gave away and the "The Box" slid into the Canadian River, tore apart, and floated downstream. It had been a profitable business and was soon rebuilt using some of the recovered lumber.

Young's Crossing was on a well-traveled north-south trail and was located in the southeastern corner of Oklahoma Territory. There were other saloons at the crossing, but "The Box" was the only one built on stilts in the river bed, and was the most popular.[2]

Neither Casey nor Powell displayed any pride in running the business nor any aptitude for bartending. During the evening of March 10, 1901, they observed that one of their customers, a John Oxley, was carrying a large roll of bills. When Casey and Powell thought that Oxley was getting ready to leave and go home, they enlisted Sam Harris, another customer, to serve at the bar. Then, they hurriedly left.[3]

Sometime later, patrons in the saloon heard shots being fired. Some of the more curious customers left the bar and started toward the direction from which the shots had sounded. They were met by an excited Charley Marshall, who had left the saloon about an hour before in the company of Rufus Choat. Marshall explained to the inquiring men that even though he and Choat lived in Indian Territory, they had left their horse and buggy on the north side of the river. When they left the saloon, they had taken home a couple of men who lived in Oklahoma Territory. After Marshall and Choat had delivered the men, they returned to the river and, while crossing it, one of the buggy shafts broke. The two men then unhooked the buggy, mounted the horse, and continued on their way home.

Charley Marshall reported that shortly after riding out of the water he heard shots fired. Their mount, burdened with both riders, fell to the ground. Marshall had not been hit by the shots, but both Choat and the horse were killed instantly. Two men, whom he assumed to be the ambushers, immediately appeared. Stunned, Charley lay still, "playing 'possum." The robbers assumed that both men were dead and scavenged the few coins which the fallen men had in their pockets.[4]

As soon as the robbers left, Marshall roused himself. He was en route to the saloon to report the murder when he met the men from the bar, who were looking for the site and purpose of the shooting.

Marshall led them a short distance to the body of Rufus Choat and the dead horse. He then pointed in the direction the killers had fled. In the sand there were two sets of footprints, plainly visible in the moonlight, which marked the murder site. One set had been imprinted by a person with oversized feet and a pigeon-toed stride, recognized by all as the footprints of Tom Powell. The other set of tracks were believed to be those of Bert Casey.[5]

Later it was learned that after Oxley had flashed his "wad of bills" in the saloon, a friend became concerned for his well-being and took him home by a different route. Choat, the mistaken victim, had been a friend of Powell's. Sam Harris (who was tending the bar at the time of the murder) reported that, later that night, Casey and Powell had told him of their crime.[6]

Rufus Choat had been murdered on the south side of the Canadian river, in the Chickasaw Nation. Tom Powell was arrested by Deputy U.S. Marshal Bob Nester. Bert Casey, however, was not available when the deputy "came calling." Casey was suspected in the crime, but he was "long gone." Powell was taken to Center (a small town six miles northwest of Ada) where he was charged with the murder and held without bond. He was later delivered to the Federal jail at Ardmore to be held until tried for the murder of Rufus Choat.[7]

Bert Casey. (Copyright, 1995, Oklahoma Publishing Company. From the September 4, 1932, issue of *The Daily Oklahoman.*)

CHAPTER 9

The Casey Gang

When Bert Casey and Tom Powell left "The Box" saloon to hijack John Oxley, they expected to find their bonanza, but the result of their effort was a total failure. Instead, they came to the sickening realization that they had killed a friend of Powell's, had obtained no money, and would now be "wanted for murder." As the situation at hand began to dawn on Bert, he left Youngs Crossing that night. Casey headed west, back to his adopted home, the Hughes ranch on the Washita River. Tom Powell had been left behind to fend for himself.

Choat may not have been the first man Bert Casey had murdered, merely his latest victim. One newspaper account of Bert's criminal career reported: "It is not generally known that Casey killed his [military] captain, in San Francisco, when he was stationed there, on the way to the Philippines. Bert was a volunteer in service, and from that time on, has followed his career of crime."[1]

Upon Bert's return to the Hughes ranch after killing Rufus Choat, he found the "welcome mat" out. Bert was soon engaged again in his chosen career, stealing. Previously, he had used whatever ranch hands he could entice to ride with him in his forays. After the murder of Rufus Choat, Bert and the Hughes ranch began to attract a more experienced lot of shady characters, men who were already following the "outlaw trail" and were "wanted by the law."

One such recruit was George Moran, a part Chickasaw Indian and a seasoned horse thief. "Walter Swofford, whose family lived near Fort Cobb, and had always been considered tough citizens," became one of Bert's allies.[2] Another was Mort Perkins, from a well-to-do Missouri family, who had run afoul of the law in Kansas City. To escape answering for his crimes in Missouri, the thirty-five-year-old Perkins came to Oklahoma Territory where he took up with Bert and became a horseback outlaw.[3]

Fred Hudson, a young man from Arkansas who was wanted for robbing the post office at Red Moon in Roger Mills County, joined the Casey gang. Ed Lockett, a whiskey peddler from Woods County, was another who pursued a criminal career in the company of Bert Casey. Jim "Bud" Sims, a horse thief from Blaine County, became a Casey gang member. Others, like Joe Mobley and Pete Williams who had no criminal record when they met Bert Casey, soon found that they too were "wanted by the law." There were many others whose names never made the newspaper and who remain unknown. This cast, the named and nameless, played roles in the Casey gang as they plundered through the Twin Territories at the beginning of the new century.

The Hughes brothers were never accused of riding with the gang, but were thought to support and provide for them. In turn, the outlaws (whom Jim and Ben referred to as their "dugout boys") did some work on the ranch, and it was assumed that the owners benefitted from the spoils of the gang's activities.

Even though Bert Casey was one of the youngest of the lot, he was the leader and the most ruthless of the bunch. The Casey gang was not a closely knit organization like the Dalton and Doolin gangs of a few years earlier. Bert had no visions of hitting a big haul, nor any aspiration to outdo any of the former outlaw leaders. His gang members were mostly small-time criminals, and Casey was too inept to plan a big job. Their specialty was stealing horses, robbing country stores, hijacking travelers, and committing other acts akin to those of a sneak thief. Casey demanded such allegiance to his leadership that frequently one or more of his men would "take out and move on," rather than accept his dictates or challenge his orders. There were rumors that Bert had killed members of his own gang when he doubted their absolute loyalty.

It was not too difficult at that time in Oklahoma Territory for "parties unknown" to steal and kill, then escape into "parts unknown" before the lawmen could get on their trail. Not only were there other outlaw havens within the area, but a chain of "hold out" places encircled the Territory. These locations were not more than a night's ride apart and were used frequently by the Casey gang.[4]

This outlaw trail provided an outlet into Kansas, where stolen horses brought ready cash, no questions asked. Throughout the Great Plains, horses were considered to be almost the same as legal tender. The demand for good animals created a profitable business for both the thief and dealer, who could dispose of the property without being caught. After selling stolen horses in Kansas, the gang frequently bartered with the same traders for other animals that had been stolen in Kansas which they could profitably dispose of in the Territory. The Casey gang also drove stolen horses south across lands of the Kiowa, Comanche, and Apache, into north Texas. Horseflesh didn't bring as much money in Texas as could be made on the Kansas market, but it was still a profitable venture.

Oklahoma Territory had been opened to homesteaders by a series of land runs. The first of these was in 1889 for the "Unassigned Lands" in what is now the central part of the state. This was followed by the runs of 1891, 1892, and 1893, for other sections of the Territory. Each of these events had created pandemonium on the day of the race. These runs had led to a multitude of personal conflicts and claim disputes, which often resulted in the death of one or both of the contenders. To preclude this massive contest of several thousand in a single horse race that created so much turmoil and conflict of claims, the authorities in Washington decided that future land openings would be conducted by lottery.

The Kiowa, Comanche, and Apache lands, along with the lands of the Caddo and Wichita, were authorized to be opened in 1901, by implementing the lottery system. Those eligible to claim a homestead could sign up after June 9, 1901, and the drawing was to be held on August 6, 1901.

As the day of the lottery approached, many of those who had registered began to flock into Lawton, the site that had been selected for the drawing. One of the interested parties who wanted to be on hand for the big event was Dr. Zeno Beemblossom of Oklahoma City. Two days before the drawing, the physician and his eleven-year-old son, Joseph Phillip ("Jay"), rode the train to Rush Springs near the western edge of the Chickasaw Nation. At Rush Springs they were met by a Professor Esly of the Tulsa Indian School, a Mr. Milder, and Harry Darbyshire, the doctor's nephew. Darbyshire was armed and provided the conveyance. The four adults and boy got into the carriage, and Darbyshire headed the team westward on the road to Lawton. After traveling an hour or so, they decided to camp early for the night, and enjoy the evening. There was no hurry as they had all of the next day to do the remaining thirty-five miles into Lawton.[5]

The influx of hopeful homesteaders gathering for the drawing provided a golden opportunity for Casey and his boys. The gang was busy hijacking the travelers en route to Lawton. Just after the Beemblossom party had pulled off the road into a grove of trees and were preparing to camp, the outlaws rode up. They shouted to the surprised campers, "Hold up your hands." There was some delay in complying with the road agents' order. One of the outlaws then yelled, "Damn 'em, if they don't get their hands up, kill 'em." An instant later a shot rang out. The bullet, which may have been intended for another of the party, took effect in the body of young Jay Beemblossom.[6]

The slug entered the boy's back close to his spine and came out near his navel, then pierced his wrist. The highwaymen

Three bandits ride into Dr. Zeno Beemblossom's camp. (Copyright, 1995, Oklahoma Publishing Company. From the September 11, 1932, issue of *The Daily Oklahoman.*)

robbed Esly, Milder, and Darbyshire of their money and personal items, then went on their way. While the doctor tended to his son, the others loaded their camp gear, hitched the team, and the party hurried back to Rush Springs. Jay Beemblossom died about midnight. The next day, Dr. Beemblossom returned to Oklahoma City with the body of his son. Jay was buried in the Fairlawn Cemetery in northwest Oklahoma City.[7]

CHAPTER 10

Chris Madsen Gets His Man

The robbery of the Beemblossom party and the murder of young Jay became popular topics of conversation among the crowds gathering in Lawton. Several other victims came forward and told of having been robbed by the trio of highwaymen. More than twenty cases of hijacking on the road to Lawton were reported. The suspects were thought to be Bert Casey, George Moran, and Mort Perkins.

Deputy U.S. Marshal Chris Madsen was near Rush Springs when he heard of the robbery and murder. He also learned that three horses had been stolen not far from where the murder had occurred. He investigated and found three spent horses in the pasture where the horses had been reported missing. Madsen presumed that the three men who had robbed the Beemblossom party and killed the boy had left their jaded mounts and ridden away on the missing horses. Checking the direction they had headed, he surmised that the wanted men had "high tailed it" for the Holt ranch, an outlaw hangout near Marlow.

As Madsen approached the Holt ranch, he learned from a nearby sharecropper that the trio had indeed been there, but had left. The farmer further advised Chris that the outlaws were going deep into the Chickasaw Nation, to George Moran's place on the Washita River, near where it empties into the Red

River. When Madsen reached Marlow, he wired fellow officers Henry A. "Heck" Thomas and William "Bill" Tilghman to meet him at Durant. He then left Marlow in his buggy and went to Ardmore, where he caught a train for Durant, the closest station to his destination.

When Chris arrived at Durant, he learned that neither Tilghman nor Thomas could join him, so he elected to proceed alone. To carry out his one-man operation, he decided to go undercover and try to get a job working on the farm directly across the road from the outlaw's place so he could watch Moran's house.

Mrs. Dollar White owned the farm where he needed to work in order to keep an eye on the outlaw's home. The only job that Mrs. White had available was picking cotton. This line of work was unbecoming to Madsen's dignity, unsuited to his rotund physique, and foreign to his natural talents, but he boasted of his aptitude and experience. She needed a "field hand" and offered him the job, which he gladly accepted. Mrs. White knew by the end of the first day that either this was Madsen's first such job or that he was too lazy to work, and so she started to terminate his employment. Realizing that he could not carry out his deception, Chris revealed to her who he was and why he was there. The widow had experienced trouble with Moran and welcomed the marshal to stay, pretend to pick cotton, and do his duty. She and her grandson who lived with her became Madsen's allies.

A few days later, as Chris was in the field groping among the cotton stalks, he was alerted by the grandson that Moran was approaching his farm. Madsen removed his Winchester from his cotton sack, crossed the road, and hid behind a log. Within a few minutes Moran appeared, driving a team of horses pulling a wagon. Madsen "got the drop" on Moran and arrested him.

With Moran handcuffed, Madsen escorted him to his captive's home. As the deputy marshal was searching Moran's abode for evidence, he detected Mrs. Moran trying to stash a pistol under a newspaper on the table, so her husband could grab it.

CHRIS. MADSEN, one of Custer Scouts, in the Seventh Cavalry. Was left for dead on battlefield of Wounded Knee. Later became Deputy U. S. Marshal, out of the Fort Smith, Wichita and Guthrie courts.

Deputy U.S. Marshal Chris Madsen. (Courtesy of Western History Collection, University of Oklahoma.)

Chris took the pistol, then found twenty watches, some jewelry, and an arsenal of guns. The deputy marshal took these items, as he considered that they were likely a part of the loot taken by the hijackers. He then arrested Moran's wife and her young brother "for harboring outlaws."

Madsen directed his three prisoners into the spring seat of the wagon, while he sat on a chair behind them with his rifle across his lap and the box of evidence at his feet. With the youth driving the team, the deputy with his three charges set off to the closest jail at Tishomingo, twenty-five miles away. A few miles up the road, Chris saw three horseback riders approaching. Their actions and the response of Moran alerted Madsen that they intended to relieve him of his prisoner. Chris ordered the boy to stop the team so he would have a steady shot while the men rode around, which they did without delay.

Madsen was tired and weary from the hours in the cotton field, arresting Moran, and traveling with his captives. When they came to a crossroads hotel, he arranged for feeding his prisoners, lodging for the night, and tending the horses. As he sat aside with his rifle, watching his prisoners while they ate, the silence at the table was finally broken. The woman quietly spoke to her husband and brother, "It's nice to eat away from home, isn't it?" Neither replied.

Madsen nailed the window shut, then allowed his three charges to go to bed in the single room. As Chris prepared to sit in the hall and guard the door, a deputy U.S. marshal entered the inn. The arriving officer was from Madill and had lost his prisoner. He volunteered to relieve the exhausted Madsen. His offer was accepted, and Chris got some much-needed rest.

The next day, as the Madill lawman was traveling with Madsen and his party, they chanced upon and recaptured his escaped prisoner. The two officers revised the seating arrangement in the wagon to provide for their additional guest, then changed their destination to Ardmore.

The one-wagon cavalcade, with its odd assortment of passengers—two lawmen who were unknown to each other, two outlaws who were strangers to each other, a boy, and a lone woman who was driving the team—arrived at Ardmore late in the evening. Upon reaching its destination the little party disbanded. The prisoners were placed in jail, Moran's wife and her little brother were released and arranged to spend the night before starting their return trip home, and the two lawmen parted to go their separate ways. George Moran, the first of the three suspects in the Beemblossom murder, was behind bars.[1]

Several months later, Deputy Marshal Madsen received a bounty for having captured George Moran. In July 1903, Auditor Baxter issued a warrant to pay Deputy Madsen the five-hundred-dollar reward.[2]

CHAPTER 11

Dr. Beemblossom
Becomes a Sleuth

The murder of his son consumed Dr. Beemblossom with vengeance. He vowed that he would do whatever was necessary to see that the guilty parties paid for their crime. He renounced his profession as a physician and immediately commenced scheming to insure that the murderers were caught.[1]

Zeno Beemblossom was of German descent. He was born in Iowa in 1855. After completing normal schooling he took some advanced courses then taught school a few terms before starting medical studies. In 1878, Zeno Beemblossom married Florence Sheppard. He graduated from the Keokuk (Iowa) Medical College in 1881 as a Doctor of Medicine. He practiced his newly earned profession in Iowa and later in Nebraska before moving to Oklahoma.

Dr. Beemblossom arrived in Oklahoma Territory on the day of the run for the Unassigned Lands, April 22, 1889, but failed to obtain a claim. About a month later he purchased the pending rights to a quarter-section of land from two contesting claimants.[2] Beemblossom homesteaded on his newly acquired claim northeast of Oklahoma Station (name later changed to Oklahoma City). He received the patent to his 160-acre homestead in 1894.[3]

He proved to be a successful farmer and stockman as well as a doctor. He purchased other farms in the immediate area of his first farm, all in the vicinity of the present-day Lincoln Park Zoo and Remington Park race track. He made improvements to the land, erected buildings, and became very prosperous. The doctor sold some of these properties in 1900, and was eager to move on to new adventures when the new lands were to open for settlement in 1901.[4] The tragedy which occurred on the road between Rush Springs and Lawton caused Beemblossom to drop all plans of expanding into the new area. He was determined to see that the parties guilty of his son's death were brought to justice.[5]

When Deputy U.S. Marshal Chris Madsen went to Durant, he thought he was on the trail of all three of the hijackers. Casey and Perkins were not with Moran when Chris found and arrested him. Moran was not inclined to provide his captor any information about his cohorts, so Madsen returned with his lone prisoner and no clue of where the other two outlaws were. Bert Casey and Mort Perkins were "long gone," and their whereabouts was unknown to the officers.

A few days after Jay Beemblossom was killed, Casey and Perkins robbed a cattleman's camp. Among the things the outlaws stole was a lady's small gold watch that had belonged to the cattleman's daughter. Perkins then visited the farm home of his sweetheart in the Chickasaw Nation and demanded that she leave the country with him. She consented, but her mother objected. Mort saddled the girl's horse, and she mounted. "They were ready to leave, when he told her to 'kiss your mother good bye; you'll never see her again.' This caused the girl to balk and dismount instantly. She defied Perkins and dared him to lay hands on her. Perkins pleaded, threatened, raged, swore and displayed a sixshooter, but the girl was the stronger in mentality of the two. She bluffed the outlaw and compelled him to ride away without her."[6]

All this time Beemblossom was on the trail of Bert Casey and Mort Perkins. He learned of the robbery of the cattleman's camp. He traced the pair of outlaws through the Chickasaw Nation, then trailed them north past Table Mountain, the Rainey Mountain School, Fort Reno, and into Kansas.

Casey had a girlfriend in one of the southern Kansas towns, where they visited a couple of days. While there, the three went to a photograph gallery and had their pictures taken. Within a few days Beemblossom acquired one of the pictures and confirmed that Casey and Perkins were two of the men who had killed his son.

Zeno Beemblossom trailed the outlaw pair southward into Kay County where Perkins had another girlfriend. He proposed marriage to her, and she consented. He gave her the lady's gold watch that he had taken from the cattleman.

Casey and Perkins became alarmed and left Kay County with Beemblossom only a two-day ride behind them. Beemblossom found where Mort's second girlfriend lived. He searched her house and found the little gold watch that Perkins had given her. From the ranch house in the Ponca country, Casey and Perkins rode the line of "hold-out" sites into Seminole country, where in the wilderness they felt perfectly secure.[7]

To what extent Beemblossom's efforts aided the officers to catch the Casey gang is not known, because the newspapers of the time did not mention his adventure into Kansas or any activity on his part. However, within two years he was credited with having done more to bring the gang to justice than any other one man.[8]

True to the vows that Beemblossom had made immediately following the murder of his son, he did not return to medicine as a profession. He established himself in the real estate business, got into politics, and worked in law enforcement. Beemblossom continued to buy, improve, and sell farms very profitably in the Oklahoma City area. He served as Oklahoma secretary of agriculture under Governor Thompson Ferguson. Even then, he continued working in law enforcement. Zeno Beemblossom was frequently assigned as a special deputy, especially on murder cases that had but few clues. When Oklahoma was granted statehood, he ran for sheriff of Oklahoma County as a Republican but was defeated.

One of his assignments as an investigative officer of the law may have been the cause of his death. A Sam Connor had been killed at a country dance at the Balzar farm home, four miles northeast of Oklahoma City (near the corner that would now be identified as N.E. 23 St. and M.L. King Ave.). Archie and Ivan Hawkins had been tried for the murder of Connor and had been acquitted. After they were freed of the charge, Dr. Beemblossom was assigned as a special deputy by Oklahoma County sheriff George Garrison to take over the investigation into the murder of Sam Connor.

J.C. Woodson had been a tenant for five years on one of the farms owned by Beemblossom; however, in December 1907, the forty-five-year-old Woodson moved to another farm. There was no known problem between the owner and the former renter. During the morning of February 18, 1908, Beemblossom went to his vacated farm. There, he found J.C. Woodson and Woodson's twenty-two-year-old son, Robert, loading some of the items that they had left behind when they had moved away. Trouble developed within the trio when the fifty-three-year-old Beemblossom objected to Robert loading a grindstone. The farm owner and the former tenant each claimed that they had purchased the item. As the older men argued, Robert proceeded to load the grindstone on their wagon. To stop Robert, Beemblossom hit him over the head with the handle of the grindstone, and they started fighting. While his son fought with the doctor, J.C. pulled a 38-caliber revolver from his coat and fired one shot into the doctor's chest. The bullet entered near his heart and Beemblossom died moments later.

The only witnesses to this killing were the Woodsons. J.C. drove to the county jail and announced to Sheriff Garrison, "I guess that you have heard of the killing, well, I am the man that did it." Officers went to the farm where the sheriff found the body of his deputy in the yard as Woodson had reported. They noted that both coats the victim was wearing were still buttoned, and his pistol was still in his pocket.

Zeno's body was delivered to the Marshall undertaking establishment. He was buried in the Fairlawn Cemetery in northwest Oklahoma City.

The newspaper article that reported Beemblossom's death

*Zeno Beemblossom, born June 13, 1855, died Feb. 18, 1908. Foreground, son "Jay,"
born July 18, 1890, died Aug. 5, 1902. Fairlawn Cemetery, Oklahoma City.* (From
the author's collection.)

provided a brief account of his life and noted that he had chased down the murderers of his son. It further stated that the doctor had recently been engaged as a special deputy in an effort to determine the person responsible for the killing of Sam Connor. The newspaper article, which was headlined "KILLS OFFICER WHO SOUGHT TO FIX A CRIME ON HIS SON," revealed that Robert Woodson was Beemblossom's main suspect in the death of Sam Connor.[9]

The first trial of the Woodsons for the murder of Beemblossom ended in a hung jury and was declared a mistrial. It was rescheduled for a later date.

At about nine-thirty on the evening of Saturday, September 18, 1910, Hubert "Bert" Beemblossom (son of Zeno), shot D.T. "Tip" Woodson, the son of J.C. and younger brother of Robert. The shooting occurred at the Austin Dance Hall, on the second floor of a building at Second and Robinson, in downtown Oklahoma City. Using the pistol that his father was carrying when he was killed, Bert fired two shots. His first hit no one, but the explosion of the cartridge set fire to the sleeve of the lady's dress with whom Tip was dancing, Olie Wagoner. Bert's second shot hit Tip in the left breast, passed near the heart, and exited his body at the left shoulder. He was rushed to the Rolator's Hospital. The first reports of his wounds indicated that his condition was critical and would likely be fatal.

Meanwhile at the dance, Bert was disarmed by a couple of men who were on the dance floor. The police arrived, arrested young Beemblossom, and led him away. Even though the band played on, the large crowd that had gathered for their popular Saturday night entertainment was soon but a mere few.

Witnesses reported that Bert had been there about an hour, and had sat quietly until he saw Woodson and Miss Wagoner dance nearby. He then stood and confronted the couple with his pistol. Olie Wagoner reported that Bert's act was caused by his jealousy of her. Beemblossom stated to the police that "while discussing the matter of a partner with a man on the dance floor, I was struck by someone on the forehead and believe it to be Woodson, with what I think was 'knucks.' You can see the

Dr. Zeno Beemblossom, right; J.C. Woodson, left; Robert Woodson, middle. (Copyright, 1995, Oklahoma Publishing Company. From the February 19, 1908, issue of *The Daily Oklahoman.*)

bruise over my eye. It stunned me and when I recovered Tip was standing in front of me. Remembering that his father had killed my father and knowing that he had it in for me because of the prosecution, I drew my gun and fired."[10]

The wound that Bert Beemblossom had inflicted on the son of his father's murderer, which was first thought would be fatal, proved not to be. Tip recovered from the gunshot, and Bert was held on the charge of "attempted murder."[11]

J.C. Woodson went on trial the second time for the murder of Dr. Z.E. Beemblossom on November 22, 1910, in Oklahoma City. J.C. took the stand and claimed that he considered it necessary to shoot Beemblossom to save the life of his son, Robert. Woodson stated "that he knew that Beemblossom had a revolver, because he was a deputy sheriff and always carried a pistol. That he had fired only after Beemblossom unloosened his overcoat and started to draw a revolver from his hip pocket." His testimony was contradictory to the evidence that Sheriff Garrison and his deputies had found at the murder site: "The victim's coats were still buttoned when they arrived." The jury was influenced by Judge George Clark's instructions which included: "A man has the right to shoot and kill in defending the life of his wife, his sons or servants." With but little deliberation, the jury reached its decision. On November 26, 1910, J.C. Woodson was found not guilty of the charge of murdering Dr. Zeno Beemblossom.[12]

The charge against Robert Woodson (J.C.'s son) for the murder of Beemblossom was dismissed on November 28, 1910. After the charges against Robert were dropped, it was rumored that Tip Woodson was willing for the charges against Bert to be dropped also and that Bert's case would be dismissed; but that did not occur, at least not at that time. The court was called to order the next morning for the trial of Bert Beemblossom for the attempted murder of Tip Woodson, with Judge Clark presiding.[13]

Two days later Judge Clark dismissed the jury when they announced that they were deadlocked and a verdict was impossible. It may be assumed that the charge against Bert Beemblossom was dropped at a later date, because no further information of this case has been located.[14]

CHAPTER 12

Two Homicides and a Hanging

George Washington Garrison, the Oklahoma County sheriff who had assigned Dr. Zeno Beemblossom to the Sam Connor murder case, was born on September 20, 1857, in Upsur County, Texas. At an early age he moved with his parents to Arkansas where young George grew up on a farm in Franklin County. In 1876, he married Martha Hunter of Charleston, Arkansas.

George had become a law enforcement officer in Arkansas, about the time that he married. When he moved his family to Texas in 1883 and settled near the boundary line between Wise and Montague Counties, he was soon designated a deputy by the sheriff of each county. While serving in that capacity he had numerous encounters with cattle rustlers and other desperadoes who swarmed in that locale. Following his exciting tenure as a dual deputy sheriff and the leader of a local vigilance committee, during which time he had succeeded in driving many of the undesirables from the community, he opened a grocery store at Sunset, Texas.

George prospered in the grocery business and in 1897 moved to Ardmore, Chickasaw Nation, and opened a large general store. Much of Ardmore, including the new general store, was destroyed by fire in June 1899, causing a great financial loss to the Garrison family. George then moved to Oklahoma City and founded the Oklahoma Saddlery Company.

In 1900, Martha, the mother of George's ten children, died. Two years later he married Kathleen Kennedy. In 1904 Garrison was the nominee of the Democratic Party for sheriff of Oklahoma County and was elected. George's constituents were well pleased with his service, and in 1907 he was re-elected to another term. His major opponent in that election had been Dr. Zeno Beemblossom, who was the Republican candidate.[1]

Three months after Deputy Sheriff Beemblossom was killed by the Woodsons, another murder occurred in Oklahoma County in which Sheriff Garrison became personally involved. Alfred "Alf" Hunter (AKA "Jim Kingsbury") and his wife (both African descendants) lived in Oklahoma City. Alf and his wife were thought to have domestic problems which frequently became violent. During the evening of May 19, 1908, Alf went to a neighbor's home on East First Street, where he thought his wife was hiding. Being refused admittance to enter, he commenced to kick in the door. Susie Pride, who lived in the house, then went out the back door and around to the front where she begged Hunter to go away. He retorted, "Damn you, I'll just shoot you," then whipped out an automatic pistol and fired six shots. Three of the bullets hit the woman, causing her instant death.

Hunter made his escape from the site before police arrived, but was seen about two hours later in the Rock Island Railroad yards. City officers and county deputies closed in on the area where several Negroes had gathered. Over a hundred shots were fired in the ensuing gun battle between the officers and the various groups of blacks who were in the Rock Island yards. No one was reported injured in this encounter during which time Hunter made his escape from Oklahoma City.

Some two weeks later Sheriff Garrison learned that a messenger had been sent by Hunter to guide his wife to his place of hiding. The sheriff got into communication with the wife and arranged with her to lead him to her husband's rendezvous.

On Friday, June 5, Sheriff Garrison, Todd Warden, a former police chief, and Deputy M.L. Saunders of Arcidia, along with

Mrs. Hunter and the guide, boarded the train at Oklahoma City. They alighted at Watonga, where they were met by Blaine County sheriff McArthur with his deputy, Billy Phillips. Mrs. Hunter and the guide were released, and they started "for the hills" with the five lawmen closely following in buggies.[2]

At a farm near Hitchcock, where the officers had been advised that Hunter was hiding, they caught sight of two Negros in a field, of whom they believed one to be Hunter. After a short chase one of the men gave up, raised his hands over his head, and walked to the posse. The officers then knew that the other man was definitely Alf Hunter, locally known as Jim Kingsbury. Sheriff McArthur and his deputy took control of the captive, whose name was Ellis, then followed Garrison, Warden, and Sanders. The officers from Oklahoma County, now on foot, were leading the pursuit and shooting at long range at the wanted man, who was running away and ducking behind the stacks of straw that spotted the wheat field. From behind one of the stacks, Hunter paused, then fired several rifle shots at the approaching officers. One of his shots hit and instantly killed Sheriff George Garrison, another wounded Deputy Sanders. Downing the two officers permitted Hunter an opportunity to escape the immediate area.[3]

When news of Sheriff Garrison's death reached Oklahoma City, a reward fund was immediately started. Hundreds of armed citizens went to the Rock Island station seeking passage to Watonga to join the search for the Negro, Alf Hunter. A special train was dispatched to deliver several of the volunteers who were accepted for the assignment. They were to present themselves to the Blaine County sheriff for service as he deemed appropriate.[4]

The Oklahoma County Commissioners immediately appointed Undersheriff Harvey D. Garrison (George's son) to the position of sheriff. All suspected hiding places throughout Blaine and Kingfisher Counties were searched extensively for Alf Hunter. Even though there were numerous reports of sighting the wanted man, he escaped the many posses in the field.[5]

The body of Sheriff Garrison was returned to Oklahoma City on Sunday morning. The funeral service, which was thought to be the largest ever in the city, was held on Monday afternoon in the First Baptist Church. Garrison was buried in the Fairlawn Cemetery of Oklahoma City.[6]

Rumors of the "wanted man" being seen in Dover, Guthrie, Oklahoma City, Kingfisher, and breaking into rural homes throughout Oklahoma were checked out. While some of these reports were likely true, Hunter could not be located by the officers in pursuit. One popular story of the time was that he had murdered two people in Arkansas before coming to Oklahoma and that Sheriff Garrison was actually his fourth victim. In spite of the best efforts of law enforcement officers, he was never found in Oklahoma.

More than a year later, Constable Augus F. McNeill of Redfield, Arkansas, began receiving information about Alf Hunter's whereabouts from a local tipster. McNeill determined that while the tips proved to be true, they were never received in time to effect an arrest. In late September 1909, he was advised that the "wanted man" was in nearby Pine Bluff, Arkansas. The constable called Deputy Sheriff W.L. Goodwin at Pine Bluff and informed him that he believed Hunter was currently in that city. The Pine Bluff officer started searching for the wanted man. McNeill then went to Pine Bluff and with the aid of Deputy Goodwin they extracted sufficient information from the tipster that enabled them to locate and arrest Alf Hunter.[7]

Communication from Governor Charles Haskell assured Governor George W. Donaghey of Arkansas that Hunter would be protected from mob violence and receive a fair trial for the murder of Sheriff George Garrison. The Arkansas governor was further assured that if Hunter was not convicted in Oklahoma, he would be returned to answer for charges pending against him in that state. Alf Hunter was then released to the Oklahoma officers, and Governor Haskell received the following message: "Requisition honored. Will be home Sunday evening with Negro. H.D. Garrison, Sheriff."[8]

Alf Hunter was delivered to the Blaine County jail. Less than three weeks after being returned to Oklahoma he was put on trial at Watonga for the murder of Sheriff Garrison. The trial lasted three days during which the accused man took the stand in his own defense. On October 16, 1909, he was convicted and sentenced to be hanged on December 3, 1909.[9]

Hunter's attorneys filed an appeal, and the sentence was postponed until the higher court reviewed the case and ruled. Alf Hunter was kept in the prison at McAlester until all legal procedures were cleared. He was returned to the Blaine County jail a few days before he was hanged at Watonga on Friday, April 8, 1910. Sheriff Harvey Garrison of Oklahoma County assisted Blaine County sheriff McArthur in carrying out the sentence. Some six minutes after the scaffold was tripped, two local doctors declared that Alf Hunter was dead. His body was taken down and turned over to the Munger Funeral Home from which it was shipped that evening under the direction of his father to the family home in Arkansas.[10]

Alf Hunter became the only person ever legally hanged in Blaine County, Oklahoma.[11]

CHAPTER 13

Caddo County Lawmen Killed

On Sunday afternoon, January 14, 1902, four boozing men loafed alongside the Washita River a short distance west of Anadarko. The river's bank, the mid-afternoon sun, and a crackling camp fire provided ample warmth to ward off the chilled air of the winter day. The remote site was suitable for their engagement. Frequent nips from the whiskey bottle propelled their gaiety and boisterous talk.

The oldest of the lot was Walter Swofford, a horse thief with a well-earned bad reputation. The leader was twenty-year-old Bert Casey, wanted for murder and an assortment of lesser crimes. The other two, Joe Mobley and Pete Williams, may have previously been involved in some minor unlawful acts, but were certainly less experienced in that field than were Casey and Swofford. The four young men spent the afternoon planning, drinking, and bragging in anticipation of the coming day, when they would pull their first bank robbery.

Casey had met Mobley and Williams at the home of Mobley's parents in the Choctaw Nation the previous Tuesday. Within a short time, Casey had the two youths anxious to follow him into his next adventure. As the trio rode from the Choctaw Nation into the Chickasaw Nation, they discussed their ambitions and agreed that a bank robbery would be a fitting project. Casey decided that the First National Bank of Mountain View would be their target.[1]

By the time the young trio reached the saloons along the Canadian River, they were ready to celebrate their expected "big haul." Casey was too well known in the area of the Corner and Youngs Crossing to visit the saloons as he was still wanted for murdering Rufus Choat at "The Box" saloon, about one year before. Mobley and Williams were unknown in the area, and they obtained a supply of whiskey, which they shared with their leader in camp.

After arriving at Anadarko they met Walter Swofford, who had been an ally of Bert in previous jobs. Casey told him of their plan to rob the bank. Swofford enthusiastically joined the party. With an ample supply of booze, the four men retired to the banks of the Washita to talk over and plot the activities of the coming day.

They decided to move out early in the evening and camp at a site closer to Mountain View, which was still twenty-five miles west. Shortly after reaching the main road, they overtook two wagons. Eager to use his new gang for whatever benefits they might gain, Casey directed that they should stop the teams and rob the people. The subdued farm families watched as the quartet of thieves searched their wagons. The robbers found but little to steal from the poor homesteaders. The outlaws spurred their mounts and disappeared from view, riding into the weakening rays of the afternoon sun. One of the victims returned to Anadarko and reported the hijacking to Caddo County sheriff Frank Smith.[2]

Smith had come to Oklahoma Territory from Denison, Texas, in 1893. He settled in Norman and was soon thereafter elected Norman city marshal. Later, Smith was appointed deputy U.S. marshal and moved to Anadarko. While serving in that deputy marshal's position in July of 1901, he was appointed sheriff of the newly formed Caddo County and proved himself to be an excellent choice for that position.[3]

Upon being advised of the roadway robbery, Sheriff Smith

rode to the site of the crime, but, by that hour, darkness prevented a search of the area. Early the next morning, he led Deputies George Beck and Will Briggs to the location. The officers were soon on the trail of the road agents. They came upon a house west of town, which the lawmen suspected was where the robbers were "holed-up."

After cautiously tying their horses some distance away, Smith stationed Briggs nearby while he and Beck approached closer to determine if the suspects were hiding in the house. As they neared the door, their hope of surprising the men while they were off guard and arresting them vanished. Suddenly, Casey's rifle thundered, sending a slug to shatter Beck's left arm. Another hit Smith in the chest. Both Smith and Beck managed to get off some shots in the direction of the abode, but they were not effective. Both officers were hit with several bullets and were dead within moments after they had approached the house. After observing his fellow officers fall and the four outlaws come out of the house, Deputy Briggs ran to his horse and "made fast tracks" for Anadarko to report the tragedy.[4]

As Smith gasped his last breaths, Casey placed his foot on the sheriff's chest and gloated over killing the officers.[5] The killers removed the weapons and valuables from the officers' bodies, then taking the lawmen's horses they headed for the Keechi Hills in the southeastern corner of Caddo County.[6]

The first officers to arrive at the murder site found the bodies of their fellow lawmen in the yard and two stray horses nearby. They assumed that the animals had been left by the escaping outlaws.[7] As the news of the double murder spread, officers and men from the surrounding area immediately armed themselves and came to Anadarko to join the search for the killers.

James S. Thompson, a cousin of U.S. Marshal Canada H. Thompson, was appointed to fill the vacancy created by the death of Smith. The new sheriff found a beehive of activity in Caddo County, as posses and individuals swarmed the area attempting to locate the outlaws. There was some speculation that the murderers were five prisoners who had recently

Frank E. Smith, born Apr. 24, 1860, died Jan. 15, 1902. I.O.O.F. Cemetery, Norman, Oklahoma. (From the author's collection.)

escaped from the prison at Leavenworth, Kansas, and were reported to be in the Territory.[8]

There were also some who thought that Ben Cravens and his gang had killed the officers.[9] Rumors had circulated that Cravens had been running with Bert Casey.[10] Since Casey was a known killer and operated in Caddo County, his gang became the prime suspects. Governor Thompson Ferguson raised the reward for the Casey gang by five hundred dollars.

One of the officers who volunteered to assist Sheriff Thompson was Neil Morrison, a former deputy sheriff of Washita County who was then city marshal of Hobart.[11] Morrison had previously encountered Casey and had a personal interest in bringing him in. Morrison led a posse into the Keechi Hills, but lost the trail and returned to Anadarko. Upon observing the horses that the outlaws had left behind at the site of the homicides, he recognized the "SB" as the brand of a ranch in the Chickasaw Nation, near Ada. He then notified A.A. "Gus" Bobbitt, an officer at Ada, about the branded horses and advised him to be on the lookout for the killers, as he thought they were headed into that area.[12]

Searches were made for the fugitives at and around the Hughes ranch, some twenty-five miles northwest of the location where Smith and Beck had been killed. No suspects were found in that area.

A few days later, two men were arrested in the northeastern part of Caddo County. They were riding toward El Reno on some horses that had been stolen a few miles east of Anadarko.[13]

Upon delivery to the Anadarko jail, these men became suspects in the killing of Sheriff Smith and Deputy Beck. After their incarceration, mob violence became a veritable threat. Sheriff Thompson displayed great leadership and bravery in protecting his prisoners and dispersing the unruly crowd. Thompson was unable to obtain any evidence to support a murder charge against the two men.

To gain information, Morrison, whose position was unknown to the prisoners, pretended to be friendly to them. When he inquired of the two inmates what they would like for him to do in their support, Gus Conger, the older of the jailed pair, asked for a gun, saying that he would do the rest. The Hobart city marshal informed the sheriff of the request. That night as Morrison went to the cell and pretended to be "ready" to slip a pistol to Conger, Thompson appeared on the scene. After confiscating the revolver, the sheriff faked an arrest of Morrison and put him in the same cell with the two men.

During the night, Conger and his companion told Morrison their story. They related that they, along with Walter Swofford and another man, had been camped in a ravine east of Anadarko making plans to rob some saloons in the area. Swofford had gone to town the previous Sunday to obtain a supply of ammunition. When Swofford, who was their leader, had not returned, the others were left in a quandary as to what to do. A short time later, the other man had left alone, and they were still in camp trying to decide a course of action when they learned of the double killing. Realizing that, if caught, they would likely be suspected of the murders, they had then stolen the horses and had set out to leave the country, when they were arrested. The next morning the sheriff pretended to release Morrison on bond.[14]

Neither officer was convinced that the two inmates had told the whole story, but did accept that they probably were not involved in killing the lawmen. The officers surmised that if the inmates' story was true, then Walter Swofford was very likely one of the men they were seeking for the hijacking and murders. To ease the anxiety of the local citizens, Thompson transferred the two prisoners to the Guthrie jail. Conger and his pal were to be held on the charge of stealing horses and be available if evidence was found to implicate them in the murders of the lawmen.[15]

The two horses that were found at the murder site, presumed to have been left by the killers, had been kept in a shed across the alley in back of the jail at Anadarko. About two weeks after Smith and Beck were killed, the horses were stolen one night. A note tacked to the jail read:

We will get a man next time
from your Esteemed Friend

Burt [*sic*][16]

After receiving the tip from Morrison about the horses' brand and the direction of the fugitives, Gus Bobbitt alerted lawmen throughout the area to be on the "look out" for the killers. Two young men were apprehended several miles southeast of Ada and delivered to Bobbitt. Governor Ferguson received a telegram from Bobbitt on February 4, 1902, advising him that he had two men in the Ada jail who were wanted for the murder of the Caddo County lawmen. "The Governor telegraphed Bobbitt instructions 'to hold the men,' then wired Sheriff Thompson 'to proceed at once to Ada and if the prisoners were the right parties, to take them into custody.'"[17]

The young men readily confessed their part in the bloody affair and, to prevent another mob threat at Anadarko, they were delivered to the Guthrie jail. While the two captives were most willing to confess their role, they refused to give their names or the names of the other two involved. They reported "that when they saw the officers ride up, they wanted to mount their horses and endeavor to escape, but the [outlaws'] leader drew his revolver and threatened them with instant death, if they did not stay and face the music." One of the young men confessed that he fired a shot or two at the time the lawmen were killed, but the other insisted that he had done no shooting.[18]

The prisoners said that "the four stayed together the first day but that night they separated, being considerably east of the Keechi hills, in a timbered country." The boys were trying to work their way back home when arrested and taken to Ada. They reported that the other two had said that "they were going to hide with friends in the rough country, to the north."[19]

Later, the prisoners acknowledged that the reason the four broke up during the first night was that they had quarreled with the leader and the man who had joined them at Anadarko. This resulted in the leader and the other man taking their guns and killing one of their horses, then leaving them on the prairie to make their getaway as best they could.

As the officers continued to question the two prisoners, they learned that their names were Joe Mobley and Pete Williams, but they were steadfast in their refusal to name the two with whom they fought. Deputy Sheriff Will Briggs was sent to Guthrie where he identified one of the young men as a participant in the killing of Smith and Beck.[20] Gus Bobbitt received the five-hundred-dollar reward for the capture of Mobley and Williams.[21]

About two weeks after Smith and Beck were killed, thirty-five county and city law officers convened at El Reno. The main subject of discussion was the recent murder of their two comrades, and how to prevent such disasters in the future. They decided to continue their all-out effort to chase the murderers to the end and capture them dead or alive. They each pledged two hundred dollars, to raise the reward offer by seven thousand dollars. They felt that this increased reward would attract still more men dedicated to the search and would insure that all of the guilty parties would be caught.[22]

CHAPTER 14

O.T. Posse Overtakes Outlaws in the Seminole Nation

About a month after Sheriff Smith and Deputy Beck were killed, the quiet little town of Asher was disturbed one evening. Asher is in extreme southern Pottawatomie County, one mile north of the Canadian River. Four strangers rode into the village and hanged a dummy in the street. "After firing several shots into it, they ran their horses out of town. The next evening, two of the men returned to Asher. This time, they walked up main street, shooting at various objects and store fronts. When they reached the end of the street, they waited at the city limits for the officers to put in an appearance. The outlaws remained for some time, but finding that they were not to be pursued, abandoned the idea of a fight and retired to the country."[1]

When Pottawatomie County sheriff Sidney Schram received information of the disturbance at Asher, he dispatched Deputy Sheriff Milner out of Shawnee to learn the details. The officer found that the random shooting had broken the windows of the Asher State Bank as well as those of the Mead and Cotton buildings. Milner contacted Sheriff Schram by telephone and reported his findings. The sheriff directed Milner to deputize as many men as he needed, then locate and arrest the troublemakers.

Deputy Sheriff George Stone of Tecumseh reached the troubled town shortly after Milner had arrived, and the two officers deputized three local citizens, Misters Mallory, Mills, and Jones. The newly formed posse soon located the camp of the suspects. They arrested Erastus Hunt and Joe King and returned them to Asher. The captured men claimed that their other two comrades had left the previous evening. The lawmen then learned that some horses had been stolen the night before from W.I. Gault, who lived near the camp where Hunt and King had been found.

The posse arrived at Gault's pasture late in the evening, located the place where the fence had been cut, and discovered the tracks of the horses which had been driven away. The prints were plain because the snow that had fallen the previous evening had ceased shortly after the horses had been taken. The posse followed this snowy trail northeast, even after they crossed from Oklahoma Territory and entered the Seminole Nation. Milner and his deputies realized that they had no authority in the Indian Territory.

The manhunters considered the situation, but on they rode, hoping to overtake the thieves and return them and the stolen horses to Pottawatomie County. The posse was also aware that they might be trailing the men who had killed officers Smith and Beck near Anadarko. Deputies Milner and Stone had been alerted, after Mobley and Williams were arrested, that the other two outlaws might be hiding in the southern part of Pottawatomie County, along the Canadian River.[2]

The realization that they were trailing an unknown number of horse thieves and perhaps killers, into an area in which they themselves had no jurisdiction, would likely have deterred veteran officers of the law. In spite of these concerns and potential pitfalls, the inexperienced but dedicated Oklahoma Territory posse continued the manhunt into the Seminole Nation.

The night was cold and still. Moonlight reflected upon the snow, and the tracks continued, plainly visible across the frozen prairie. From time to time the riders dismounted and walked, to warm their bodies and relieve their horses. The lawmen were still on the trail when just before daybreak on Friday, February

21, 1902, they came upon a large corral and two small barns. The tracks that they had followed throughout the night led to the corral, and they could see several horses enclosed. Some distance away was a log cabin and a tent set up near it.[3]

The posse left their horses in some trees, then posted themselves in the barn and behind the large corral posts to apprehend the thieves when they came to "tend the stock." The hidden officers had waited but a few minutes when a boy came out of the cabin and, while "looking all around," ambled to the corral and entered. Deputy Milner ordered him to "go to the barn and halt, that he would be killed if he ran or made a noise." The lad immediately obeyed.

Soon thereafter, two men carrying half-filled sacks of corn came out of the house and walked toward the corral. As they approached, the lawmen could see that they were armed. After they entered the horse pen, Milner ordered them to "throw-up-your-hands." Both men dropped the bags of horse feed. One started a move for his pistol, but glimpsing the barrel of a nearby well-aimed rifle, did not proceed. They too, were directed to advance to the barn. With some delay and oaths of contempt, they reluctantly started. The action in the corral had been seen by the people in the house.[4]

Two men rushed from the cabin and while shooting at the officers ran toward the corral. One of the men sought shelter behind a lone tree, standing directly between the lawmen and the house. The other man ran at an angle and dropped behind a slight embankment near the woods. Rifle shots were rapid and plentiful, as three deputies returned fire at the two outlaws. Two of the posse who were in the barn concerned themselves with guarding the three captives until they could disarm the two men. A shot fired by one of the hiding outlaws hit Deputy Stone in the groin, and he went down.[5]

The lawmen continued to fire, placing slug after slug into the protections of the attackers. The tree did not provide a full shield for the hiding gunman, and while levering in another shot, he exposed his side. A bullet entered under his arm, and he fell to the ground. More of the lawmen's bullets found their mark, and he lay motionless. The officers then concentrated on the man in the ditch, who also had a disadvantaged position. As the tempo of their shots increased, the lone resisting outlaw started crawling down the shallow wash on his stomach. When he reached the trees, he jumped up and ran into the woods.[6]

The officers secured their prisoners, checked the wound of Deputy Stone, and confirmed that the outlaw at the tree was dead. Remembering the recent demise of the officers in Caddo County, Deputy Milner stayed his men at that point. Fearing that more outlaws might be in the cabin waiting to ambush them, or attack the guards if they split their four-man force, the posse did not approach the house or pursue the escaping gunman. They fired their arms from some distance away and riddled the tent, in case some of the thieves were hiding there.

The posse loaded their wounded comrade, their two prisoners, and the dead outlaw into a wagon (the boy was not taken), then hitched up a team and made their way north. They traveled about ten miles to reach Wewoka, capital of the Seminole Nation. A surgeon removed the bullet from Deputy Stone which had fractured his hip. The captured men were placed in jail, and the dead outlaw was delivered to a funeral home, where the body was to be embalmed and held for identification.[7]

Upon receiving word from Deputy Milner of the posse's adventure and accomplishments, Sheriff Schram immediately went to Wewoka. He identified the dead outlaw as Walter Swofford, who had on occasion been an inmate in the county jail at Tecumseh. There was much confusion as to the identities of the captured men. The early accounts reported them to be Bert Casey and Bill Watson, a fugitive from Kentucky charged with murder. The two prisoners were later correctly identified as Mort Perkins, wanted for the Beemblossom murder, and Sam Cooper, who was also wanted in Oklahoma Territory on other charges. Bert Casey, the young leader of the gang who was wanted on at least three murders charges and numerous other crimes, had again escaped. It was later determined that he was the one who had crawled down the ditch and run away.[8]

Officers recovered twelve horses from the corral, one had been killed during the gun battle. They also recovered fifteen saddles, five sets of nearly new harness, four good buggies, hundreds of rounds of ammunition, and dozens of Winchesters and six-shooters, among them one with a scabbard that had belonged to Sheriff Smith.[9]

The lawmen learned that "two women, soiled doves of the vicinity, had spent the night with Casey and Swofford, in the tent and were still there when the shooting started. Notwithstanding the fierceness of the fight and that the tent was riddled with holes, the women remained there until the battle was over. An examination of the tent afterward and the remarks of the women proved that some of the bullets passed within six inches of them."[10]

Sheriff Schram traveled to Guthrie and secured requisition papers to return the prisoners and the dead outlaw to Oklahoma Territory. Swofford's relatives were notified. Perkins and Cooper were delivered to the Federal jail at Guthrie.[11]

"The Pottawatomie County posse that effected the raid on the outlaw camp received the plaudits and congratulations of all good citizens."[12] "The officers which had no previous experience as manhunters, accomplished a telling blow on outlawry in the Territories. They would, without doubt receive the outstanding rewards, which was speculated to be as much as nine thousand dollars."[13]

"Sheriff Thompson and the people of Caddo County praised the posse highly." Bert Casey's escape was the only shortcoming of the endeavor. Disappointment that Casey had gotten away prompted one editor to expound upon his character as follows: "There is no doubt that Casey, when cornered, is a coward and is as craven as is possible to be. He, while posing as the leader of the gang, made each take a solemn oath to fight to the death, yet in a pinch, he was the only one to sneak away on all fours in the brush, leaving his brave and nervy partner, Swofford dying with six bullets in his body."[14]

By arrangement Arthur Swofford, Walter's younger brother, met the officers at Shawnee when they returned with the outlaw's body. Arthur identified the remains as that of his brother, Walter. A dispatch from Governor Thompson Ferguson announced that "the identification of Swofford's body was satisfactory" and directed the officers to "turn the remains over to his relatives for internment."[15]

Apparently, Arthur Swofford soon took up his older brother's bad habits. About a year after Walter was killed, Arthur was arrested in Oklahoma City and charged with "larceny of a horse" in Washita County.[16]

CHAPTER 15

Murder on Dead Indian Creek

During the morning of June 30, 1902, Roger Mills County sheriff Andrew Jackson "Jack" Bullard was advised that there were some suspicious characters camped north of town. Sheriff Bullard learned from the informer that the party consisted of one man about forty years old, another about twenty years old, two young boys, and a woman with two small children, seven persons in all. They were reported to be well armed and in possession of a mixed lot of livestock and saddles, which they were trying to sell in the neighborhood.

That afternoon, Sheriff Jack Bullard and Deputy Sheriff John Cogburn left Cheyenne, the Roger Mills County seat, to check on the reported suspicious operation. The lawmen located the camp of the reported parties on Dead Indian Creek, near the Day County line.[1]

The older man, who weighed about two hundred pounds, introduced himself to the officers as Sam Green and presented the woman as his wife with their two children. Green reported that he had been employed on a ranch in Woodward County and was moving west. The clean-shaven young man, who was about five feet eight inches tall and weighed about one hundred and sixty pounds, was introduced as Pete Whitehead. Contrary to his name, he had dark hair.

Main street, Cheyenne, Oklahoma Territory, circa 1902.
(Courtesy of Western History Collection, University of Oklahoma.)

While the lawmen were conversing with Green and White-head, Frank Doan rode up. Bullard recognized Doan as a local rancher in the community. The sheriff called Doan off to the side and inquired of him what he knew about the parties being questioned and of their activities. While Bullard and Doan were talking some distance from the others, they observed White-head hand Green a six-shooter and saw the two boys disappear behind a ridge. After a short discussion with the sheriff, the local rancher mounted his horse and departed. He had ridden about a quarter of a mile when he heard several shots being rapidly fired. Looking back at the camp, Doan saw amid the gunsmoke one man fall and another run toward his horse.[2]

Frank Doan recruited a neighbor, Joe Means, and together they captured Mrs. Green, her two children, and one of the growing boys.[3] As neighbors in the area came to the scene, they found that Sheriff Bullard had been shot eleven times, with three different caliber of guns, including one that fired an explosive bullet. Bullard's pistol was in his hand and two shots had been fired from it. Apparently Deputy Cogburn had been sitting on the wagon tongue when the shooting started. He received only one shot and it was in the back. It must have taken effect immediately, as Cogburn's pistol was still holstered. Before making their escape, the killers had removed the sheriff's rifle from his saddle scabbard and had taken it with them.

"The outlaws had in their possession three wagons, twenty-one head of horses, fourteen head of cattle [only two of the animals were branded alike] and a lot of miscellaneous articles. Three of the horses were recognized, as belonging to a Mr. Hex of Greer County, one was a racer. It was presumed that White-head and Green thought that the Sheriff had sent Doan for help and that he intended to arrest them. To save themselves from capture, they concluded to murder both men before help could arrive. They must be desperados of the worst type."[4]

When word of the disaster reached Cheyenne, a posse was formed, and they went to the campsite. The posse brought the bodies of Bullard and Cogburn to town where they were laid out in the courthouse.[5] The Masonic Lodge of Cheyenne conducted the funeral of Sheriff Bullard, who was buried in the local cemetery. It is thought that Deputy Cogburn's body was taken to Martha, a small town near Altus, for burial.

The woman, her two children, and the boy, Otis Stuhl, were delivered to the Roger Mills County jail. She maintained that she was the wife of Sam Green. She claimed that the shooting occurred because the officers called her a thief and outlaw, and that the men of the party fired on the lawmen to protect her honor. Little credence was given to her story. Mrs. Green, her children, and Stuhl were held as accomplices to the murders.[6]

The two gunmen, who were identified as Green and Whitehead, made good their escape. They left the scene riding northwest, then looped around and headed in the opposite direction. They were reported to have been seen the next day about twenty-five miles southeast of Cheyenne, near Elk City.[7]

One newspaper speculated that "while it is not positively known who composed the gang of outlaws, yet suspicion points to the Bert Casey gang, as they have been operating in that portion of the Territory."[8]

A short time after the Roger Mills County officers were killed, Temple Houston, a popular Woodward attorney, offered to bring in Green and Whitehead if the county would grant them release on bond. Temple was the youngest son of Sam Houston, the founder of the Texas Republic. He was well on his way to a life of politics in Texas when Oklahoma Territory was opened for settlement. Young Houston decided to stake his claim in the "new country" rather than remain under the shadow of his father in Texas. He settled in Woodward and commenced practicing law in several of the northwestern counties of the Territory. His involvement in the gunfight that occurred at Woodward in 1895, with John and Ed Jennings in which Ed was killed, had not damaged but rather had enhanced his career.

Houston was a frequent visitor at Cheyenne, where he had been the attorney for the defense in several trials. The county officials could not accept the idea of releasing the murderers on bond. They never learned if Houston could have actually produced the wanted men, because his offer was rejected.[9]

Temple Houston enjoyed great respect throughout the Territory and undoubtedly would have emerged as one of Oklahoma's prime leaders during the formative years of the state had not fate determined another course. Three years after Temple negotiated with the Roger Mills County officials in behalf of the two suspects, he became ill. The popular forty-five-year-old attorney died of a brain hemorrhage two years before Congress granted statehood to the Twin Territories. Years later, Temple served as the pattern for Edna Ferber's leading character Yancy Cravat in her popular novel *Cimarron*.[10]

The search for Green and Whitehead continued. Deputy Sheriff Neil Morrison reported that he and Sheriff John Miller of Washita County had led a posse to the Hughes ranch, east of Cordell. "With a posse, we surrounded the ranch, after making sure that Bert Casey was there, also that Ben Williams, alias Whitehead, the man wanted for murdering Sheriff Jack Bullard and a deputy of Roger Mills county, a short time ago was with him. During the night Jim Hughes slipped past our guards and notified the gang that the place was surrounded. Casey, Williams and another man slipped away and escaped."[11]

Roger Mills County sheriff Elliott received word in August 1904 that Sam Green and Pete Whitehead were being held in a North Dakota jail. His trip to return the "wanted men" to Oklahoma Territory became a futile effort, as the information proved to be erroneous. In September 1905 he went to Portland, Oregon, on a like mission, again with the same result. Sheriff Elliott's pursuit of the wanted men took him to Vancouver, British Columbia, in May 1906. Information was received at Cheyenne that he had the men located and extradition papers were being prepared in Washington for their return to Oklahoma Territory.[12] Again, something must have failed to materialize, as subsequent newspapers of Roger Mills County for the following weeks do not mention that either of the suspects was brought in. No one was ever tried for the murders of Sheriff Jack Bullard and Deputy John Cogburn.[13]

Mrs. Green and Otis Stuhl were held in the Roger Mills County jail for several months, then were released for lack of evidence. Stuhl and Mrs. Green with her two children were delivered to Enid, the county seat of Garfield County.[14]

About forty years after the tragedy on Dead Indian Creek, a dam was constructed which backed up the water and formed a popular recreational lake. The lake was named for the creek and is near the site where the horse thieves were camped and the officers were killed.

CHAPTER 16

"Get Bert Casey"

When Canada H. "Harry" Thompson was appointed U.S. marshal of Oklahoma Territory in 1897, he selected William D. "Bill" Fossett to be his chief deputy. Bill Fossett lived at Kingfisher and had been a railroad detective for the Rock Island Line. The marshal's annual salary had recently been raised to five thousand dollars, and the salary for the chief deputy had been increased to fifteen hundred dollars per year.

The previous marshals had been credited with making great strides in wiping out the outlaw gangs that had infested Oklahoma and Indian Territories. Notorious outlaw gangs of the area were practically exterminated with the demise of the Dalton, Doolin, Cook, and Buck gangs. The Jennings gang surfaced soon after Thompson became marshal, but their tenure as outlaws was short-lived. Not long after Thompson took office, the last members of the old Doolin gang who were still "at large," Dynamite Dick Clifton and Little Dick West, were done in. Individual longtime lawbreakers like Ben Cravens and Jim Harbolt continued to present frequent and major problems for the Territorial lawmen.

By 1900, the sheriffs and their deputies of Washita, Caddo, and Kiowa counties had become familiar with the name of Bert Casey. He had often been suspected of stealing horses and of committing numerous other crimes. Casey had escaped all attempts to locate and arrest him. After the murder of Rufus Choat in March 1901, Casey was regarded as also being a killer. The murder of Jay Beemblossom in August 1901 added to Casey's notoriety. Rufus Choat had been killed across the river in the Chickasaw Nation, but Jay Beemblossom had been slain in the newly opened area of Oklahoma Territory, which prompted greater concern by the U.S. marshal's office at Guthrie. The search for Bert Casey brought more attention to the Hughes ranch, where he was believed to "hide out." Ben and Jim Hughes denied any knowledge of Casey's criminal activities or his whereabouts.

Less than a month after the outlaw trio had robbed the Beemblossom party and killed young Jay near Rush Springs, Casey again made the newspapers. Washita County sheriff John Miller received word that three mules and a buggy had been stolen from a farm near Odessa, in the southern part of the county. He sent Deputy John K. Bottom to investigate.

"Deputy Bottom soon struck the trail of the robbers and followed it north into the Hughes ranch. At that point, and before he anticipated any action, Bert Casey and another man 'threw down' on him with rifles. They disarmed the deputy and held him prisoner. He was taken down to the river and threatened that they would tie a weight to his neck and throw him in. After intimidating Deputy Bottom about four hours they returned his pistol, but kept his ammunition and Winchester, then released him. The other man was a stranger to the officer."

The article continued: "Had Bottom made any demonstration, no doubt that he would have been killed. The citizens of that community are getting pretty well aroused over the affair and if Casey and his pal are caught, 'Judge Lynch' is liable to be called in. There is very strong sentiment against the Hughes brothers for harboring such men, and they are liable to be handled rather roughly."[1]

A few days later, Washita County deputy sheriff Neil Morrison and a small posse found Bert Casey at the Hughes ranch and arrested him. As they approached Cloud Chief with their prisoner, they were fired upon by five men. Casey was shot in the shoulder but managed to escape. Morrison later explained "that Casey had smallpox at the time, and this fact allowed him the latitude that enabled him to make his get away." Morrison continued: "This is the worst gang in Oklahoma, but the members can be run to earth, if the federal and territorial authorities will co-operate. Casey has sworn to have my life, but if he gets me he will have to beat me to the gun."[2]

During the first week of November 1901, four men held up the post office and a store at Korn (spelling changed to Corn in 1918), in northeastern Washita County. The double robbery netted them about one hundred and fifty dollars. Two of the thieves were recognized as Bert Casey and Ben Cravens. Four days later, four men held up two stores at Colony, eight miles southeast of Korn. They got fifty dollars from the Seger store, but nothing at Crawford's store. Again, two of the robbers were identified as Bert Casey and Ben Cravens.[3]

On New Years day 1902, Chief Deputy U.S. Marshal Bill Fossett and Washita County sheriff John Miller led a posse of fifty men in a raid on the Hughes ranch. They hoped to surprise and capture Casey and his cohorts. The gang had obviously been tipped off, and Fossett's posse came up empty handed.

While the raid at the Hughes ranch proved to be fruitless, a small posse led by Deputies Bottom and Griffin located Levi Reed and Jim Sims and arrested them. Reed and Sims (two of the Casey gang) were found at a Mrs. Vest's place three miles south of Cordell. The two outlaws were heavily armed and attempted to run, but when they realized that they were surrounded, they reluctantly surrendered. The captives were handed over to Marshal Fossett. Reed was wanted for stealing horses in Kiowa country (prior to it being opened for homesteading) and escaping from the Guthrie jail. Sims was wanted for stealing horses in Woods County and breaking out of the Blaine County jail at Watonga. Fossett returned Reed to the Guthrie jail and turned Sims over to the Blaine County sheriff.[4]

Jim Sims had been back in jail only three days when, on January 5, 1902, he led another breakout from the Blaine County jail. He and four other inmates escaped, taking the jailer, Deputy Sheriff Richardson, as their hostage. They left the deputy two miles south of Watonga near the North Canadian River, as they hastened on their way. Richardson managed to loosen the ties that bound him, then walked back to town.

Some of the prisoners who were in jail on minor charges did not take the freedom offered by the five, but stayed behind when the escapees left with the deputy as their hostage. The town learned of the escape from the inmates who remained in jail before the jailer made his way back from the river. Over an hour had passed before a search for the escapees was started. The posse was unable to locate any of the wanted men.[5]

Only two weeks after Chief Deputy Fossett led the raid on the Hughes ranch in search of the young outlaw, Casey struck again. The murders of Sheriff Smith and Deputy Beck of Caddo County on January 15, 1902, increased the clamor of the citizens in calling for the lawmen to "get Bert Casey."

Only slight relief was provided a month later, when on February 21, Deputy Sheriff Milner and a posse trailed some stolen horses into the Seminole Nation. They located the horse thieves south of Wewoka and in the ensuing gunfight killed Walter Swofford and captured two of the outlaws. Casey's cowardly escape from that encounter added to his despicable reputation.

In March 1902, an old man by the name of Arnold was shot in the head and killed. When found several days later, his body was in a bad state of decomposition. His shallow-buried remains had been unearthed and partially eaten by hogs. Arnold lived alone near Homer, a small town in the vicinity of Ada. Bert Casey's maternal grandparents lived close to Arnold's place, and it was known that Bert occasionally stayed at his grandparents' home. Robbery was the obvious motive for the crime, and Bert Casey was thought to be the killer.[6]

When President William McKinley took office in 1901, he appointed Harry Thompson to another term as U.S. marshal of Oklahoma Territory. McKinley was assassinated a short time after taking office, and Vice President Theodore "Teddy" Roosevelt ascended to the presidency. In the spring of 1902, Thompson resigned from his position, and Roosevelt appointed Bill Fossett to be the new U.S. marshal of Oklahoma Territory. Having served as chief deputy, Fossett was well aware that the most urgent problem facing him and Oklahoma lawmen at the time was Bert Casey.

The murders of Sheriff Bullard and Deputy Cogburn in Roger Mills County on June 30, 1902, brought forth another outcry to "get Bert Casey and wipe out the Hughes ranch." A few days later, Sheriff Miller and Deputy Morrison led a posse to the Hughes ranch, in search of the lawmen's killers. The officers did find and arrest Andrew Lanhan, Claude Powers, and Levi Reed (the man Fossett had returned to the Guthrie jail, following his raid at the Hughes ranch on New Years day 1902). The three men who were arrested were "wanted by the law" but were not the prime targets. Casey had again escaped, which prompted Deputy Morrison to go to Guthrie and try again to obtain more active support from Fossett's office. He solicited the marshal's help in trying to catch "the gang of murderers and horse-thieves that was known to rendezvous at the Hughes ranch."[7]

In late July 1902, Caddo County officers thought they had Casey and some of his gang located in a dugout on the Hughes ranch. They sent word from Cloud Chief to Mountain View and Anadarko, asking for volunteers to come and assist in capturing the gang. Able-bodied men from throughout the area responded. They loaded their weapons and rode to the ranch alone and in groups. Sheriff Miller and the men (estimated at sixty to seventy) closed in on the site and arrested Jim Hughes, Jim Haley, and four others. They were certain that Casey had been in the immediate area shortly before the raid, but he couldn't be located. They found boot prints that were thought to be his and followed them to and along the river, where they disappeared. Casey had escaped again. A pair of stolen mules was found at the ranch. Jim Hughes and the other five men who had been arrested were taken to the Cordell jail.[8]

As more efforts of the combined local tri-county law enforcement officers failed to bring in Bert Casey, the pressure on Marshal Fossett increased. The young outlaw had escaped from his only arrest before the officers could get him in jail. The only accomplishment by the U.S. marshal's force to bring in any of the Casey gang had been Chris Madsen's arrest of George Moran. Fossett's own raid on New Year's day 1902 had been a failure. The marshal realized that he must take action to "get Bert Casey."

To cope with the Casey problem, Fossett decided to follow the advice of the old adage that "it takes a thief to catch a thief." At that time, in the Federal jail at Guthrie, were inmates who had ridden with Bert Casey and knew his contacts and hideouts. The marshal discussed his plan with the head jailer, Deputy J.L. McCracken. They decided that one prisoner, a Fred Hudson who was being held on charges of robbing a post office, would be a fitting man for the anticipated job. The officers discussed with Hudson the idea of rejoining the Casey gang, then at the earliest opportunity of bringing Bert in "dead or alive."

Hudson had no qualms nor hesitancy about accepting the assignment, if arrangements could be made to meet his terms, which were that he be: released from the charges pending against him, deputized as a U.S. marshal, assured the right to receive all rewards, and granted the release of one prisoner to accompany him. Marshal Fossett and jailer McCracken accepted the prisoner's stated conditions. Hudson selected fellow inmate F.M. "Ed" Lockett, who was charged with selling whiskey, to be his accomplice. There could be no schedule established for such an undertaking, but the four men discussed the matter and mutually anticipated that the mission could be accomplished within thirty days. After assuring Marshal Fossett that they would bring Casey in, "one way or the other," the two inmates were released, deputized, armed, and sent on their way in late August 1902.[9]

After Hudson and Lockett were dispatched, other deputies were deployed to the Anadarko area, to be nearby if their assistance was needed in the anticipated showdown with Bert Casey. Weeks passed and the only information received at Marshal Fossett's office indicated that the Casey gang was still in full operation. Crimes were routinely being reported, and Bert Casey was usually the first person suspected.

A deputy sheriff in the northern part of Caddo County trailed Casey and his gang to a canyon northwest of Binger, on October 2, 1902. A number of hastily summoned deputies and farmers formed a picket line around the chasm, which was described as a half-mile long, two hundred yards wide, and about two hundred feet deep. The canyon was on the open prairie, but the lower elevation was covered with trees and brush. Sheriff Thompson and several officers departed from Anadarko on a special train. Upon the sheriff's arrival at the site, they attacked the outlaw camp. The surrounded men soon realized that they were at the mercy of the well-armed posse who were firing from above, and so the outlaws surrendered. "When the shooting started, Casey abandoned his companions, then leaving his horse, crawled on his hands and knees out of the canyon and escaped again."[10]

Two days after the capture of six of Casey's men in the canyon near Binger, a train robbery was attempted south of Chickasha. A Rock Island passenger train was attacked at the same location where the Jennings gang had robbed a train a few years earlier. In the recent attempt, a volley of bullets crashed through the sides of the cars as the train approached siding No. 1. "The engineer refused to heed the attack, but put on more steam and sped the train on." Only one passenger was injured, having been struck in the eye with a piece of flying glass. "It is believed that the attack was made by Bert Casey and some of his men that he joined after escaping from Sheriff Thompson's posse at the canyon."[11]

In late October a banker at Rush Springs was robbed and his horse stolen. Suspicion naturally fell on the Casey gang.

Two months had passed and Marshal Fossett had received no word from the prisoners whom he had released from jail, with only their promise to bring in the young outlaw. Instead of having the outlaw Bert Casey behind bars or in the cemetery as Fossett had planned, he was actually missing two inmates. The marshal surely pondered: had the freed men simply grabbed the chance and left the country, instead of carrying out their assigned duties as his special deputies? Marshal Fossett was undoubtedly having second thoughts about his chosen method of using prisoners for the task and of the men he had selected and deputized to "get Bert Casey."

CHAPTER 17

The Moment of Truth
at Cleo Springs

Anxiety had risen in the marshal's office because of Fossett's concern over not having received any information from his two special deputies. About noon on Monday, November 3, 1902, the uncertainty of his venture to "get Bert Casey" cleared with the arrival of a message. A telegram was received from Hudson and Lockett, which simply stated that Casey and Sims had been killed, then inquired of the marshal what he wanted done with the bodies. The inspired account of recent events that was reported by Marshal Fossett to *The Weekly Oklahoma State Capital* (which appeared in the November 8, 1902 issue of that Guthrie newspaper) reveals his relief and excitement:

"The greatest nerve ever displayed and certainly the most that I have ever heard of was that of the four men, in hand to hand fight over the camp fire, between the two deputy marshals, Lockett and Hudson, and the two outlaws, Sims and Casey," said United States Marshal Bill Fossett yesterday afternoon to the State Capital man, after the officers had returned to Guthrie, bringing with them the body of Bert Casey. In the party of officers arriving in Guthrie with the body, were United States Marshal Bill Fossett, Federal Jailer J.L. McCracken, and Deputy Marshals Fred Hudson and Ed Lockett. They had left the body of Jim Sims, the

other outlaw, at Watonga, turning it over to Sheriff Bridge-
ford, from whom Sims had escaped last spring.

"About two months ago," continued Marshall Fossett,
"with Jailer McCracken, we fixed the scheme to get possession dead or alive, of Bert Casey, the leader of the gang of
outlaws. We chose Fred Hudson and Ed Lockett to do the
work and immediately started them out to get the outlaw
and whatever other men were with Casey at the time. Both
Hudson and Lockett were deputized as marshals and [sent
out] to ascertain the whereabouts of Casey.

"At that time, Casey, they ascertained was out of the territory, but within a few weeks they fell in with him and Jim
Sims and have since been with them as members of the
Casey gang. Hudson knew both of them before and the
opportunity to of [sic] getting two recruits was considered
a good one by Casey. Back and forth over the country they
traveled for some time, small job crimes being committed,
but at no time could the two deputies get the opportunity
to arrest their man.

"When on their scout about two weeks ago, Sims went to
Rush Springs, I.T., where he held up a banker of that City,
compelled him at the point of a gun to lead his fine gray
made [sic] to the outskirts of the town and then turn her
over to Sims who rode her away. She was recovered yesterday, by Marshal Fossett at the outlaws' camp near Cleo
Springs.

"A short time ago Casey determined upon the plan to
rob the bank at Cleo, in Woods county, and sent Lockett
and Hudson ahead to look the ground over and report on
the feasibility of the plan. Casey was always the boss in
camp and did all planning of the crimes to be committed.
None of his men ever crossed him. Hudson and Lockett
reported adversely on the Cleo bank robbery to Casey and
Sims, when they arrived in the neighborhood, and the four
went into camp in a pasture, near Cleo Springs, on the
night before the fight took place between the two outlaws
and the two officers.[1]

"On that evening, while alone, Hudson and Lockett
devised a plan for Casey's arrest. Hudson said to Lockett—

'For several weeks we have been with these men, whom we have sworn to arrest, and as yet we have never been able to get between Casey and his gun. There have been many times, when he was in bed and we were also, that we could have killed him, but this we did not want to do.'

"Then Hudson proposed this plan—'In the morning, after we have had a good night's rest, we will prepare breakfast and wash the dishes. Then you sit down across the camp fire from Sims and I will sit down across from Casey. We will take our guns from our belts, warm them over the fire to see that they are in good working order, do it leisurely so that they will not suspect, and when I nod my head, you throw down on Sims and tell him to put up his hands, for at the same time I will throw down on Casey. We will take them alive if possible, and if not we will have a fair, square out of it.'

"The plan worked. The breakfast was prepared and the dishes washed, after both Lockett and Hudson had secured the good night's sleep both needed after weary marches. Both men took their positions at the fire, as prearranged and both warmed their guns over the fire, cocking and recocking the weapons to see that they were in good working order. Suddenly Hudson nodded his head toward Lockett and at the same moment threw down on Casey and told him to throw up his hands. Casey immediately went for his gun, but Hudson again warned him that to pull the gun would mean instant death.

"Casey had often declared that he would never be taken alive, so he pulled the gun. Both men shot at the same time, but fortunately for Hudson, the bullet from Casey's gun went wild, while his own took effect in the outlaw's body. Casey shot again as he fell backward and Hudson shot twice more, every bullet taking effect.

"In the meantime Lockett was having it out with Sims, who proved to be as brave as Casey. Both of the outlaws had pulled their guns at the same time, but Lockett who had Sims covered, did not shoot until he saw what Casey would do. This gave Sims an opportunity to kill Lockett, which he was not slow about attempting. He pulled the trigger of the weapon back, but it refused to fall again, and that saved Lockett's life and probably Hudson's also.

"Seeing that Sims would kill him, Lockett fired at the same time as Sims attempted to do, and killed the outlaw. The whole circumstance did not cover a minute's time, but it was sufficient to rid the country of two of the worst outlaws in the records of the territory.

"Immediately after the fight Hudson and Lockett notified a nearby farmer, told him they were officers sent to arrest the outlaws and that they had killed them in attempting to arrest them. They requested the farmer to go to Cleo immediately and have officers from there come to the scene of the shooting. This was done and the news of the killing of the outlaws spread like wild fire.

"Within a short time the entire neighborhood had assembled at the place and immediately a rejoicing took place, such as was never known there before. The bodies of the dead men were kept there until the arrival of myself and McCracken, when we immediately started for Guthrie with the body of Casey, the sheriff of Blaine County having requested the body of Sims. I have never known or heard of such nerve before as was displayed around that camp fire at Cleo. The story of Hudson and Lockett, by the way, is verified by a farmer, on whose land the killing occurred. He was hunting his cattle and happened upon the camp as the fighting was taking place."[2]

The article went on to say that "Hudson and Lockett are entitled to every cent of the reward offered for Casey, dead or alive, and for Sims, although the latter may be small. It is estimated that the rewards on Casey's head averaging from $3,000 to $9,000. There is no doubt that the two deputies will get this reward money. It is offered by the governor, by the marshal, by the sheriffs association of Oklahoma, and by friends of murdered men."[3]

The marshall ended his report of the gunfight by extolling the bravery of his deputies and basking in their accomplishments: "When the two outlaws were killed there was but four or five feet of space between them and the officers. All men were determined to fight to the death. They knew that it meant the death of at least two of them, and the fight was desperate."

The article listed Casey's crimes as including "murder, highway robbery, bank robbery, stage robbery and almost every other crime on the calendar." It reported that "he was considered the most dangerous and unprincipled bandit of the present day, always killing when an opportunity presented itself."

It also advised that Bert Casey's body was being held at the morgue of "the Patterson undertaking establishment" in Guthrie for further identification and to await claim by relatives. Dr. Beemblossom identified Casey's body as that of his son's murderer. Washita County deputy John Bottom, who had encountered Casey eight months earlier, identified the body. Officer Bud Griffin of Cordell, who had known Casey for several months, also confirmed the identification.[4]

Bert Casey was described as not a large boy, and would not have been twenty-one years old until sometime in December. It appeared that Casey had dyed his hair red a few weeks before, as the ends were red but the rest was a natural brown. He had about eighty dollars on his person at the time of death. Sims was described as a large man, with a beard, and as "rough looking."[5]

The description given of Pete Whitehead (the younger of the two men who were wanted for the murder of Sheriff Bullard and Deputy Cogburn) was compatible with that of Bert Casey except for the color of hair. Had Casey dyed his brown hair black, to help cover his identity, while traveling with Green and using the name Whitehead? Had he then applied the red dye to change his dark hair, after killing officers Bullard and Cogburn?

Stealing and selling horses was Casey's most routine and frequently repeated crime, the same operation the men who identified themselves as Green and Whitehead had been engaged in at the time they killed the Roger Mills County officers. If Fred Doan (who had witnessed the murders) had been sent to Guthrie, would he have recognized the body of Bert Casey as the young man called Whitehead in camp on Dead Indian

Creek? There were numerous reports that Pete Whitehead was part of the Casey gang. His being known by some as Bert Casey and by others as Pete Whitehead would lead to the assumption that there were two separate people, but were they?

The officials contacted Casey's relatives, as they thought that George W. Casey or some of his kin would claim the body of Bert. Apparently none did, and he was buried on November 8, 1902 (incorrectly applied to his tombstone as the date of his death), in the "boot hill section" of the Summit View Cemetery at Guthrie. His resting place is beside those of Little Dick West, Bill Doolin, Charlie Pierce, and other notorious horseback outlaws of Oklahoma Territory.[6]

Bert Casey, killed Nov. 8 [sic Nov. 3], 1902 by U.S. Marshals. Summit View Cemetery, Guthrie, Oklahoma. (From the author's collection.)

CHAPTER 18

Deputy Lute Houston, a Victim of the Noose

In the interview that U.S. Marshal Fossett conducted with newspaper reporters about the deeds of his two special deputies at Cleo Springs, he did not mention that besides Hudson and Lockett, a third special deputy had been assigned to the case. About a month after Hudson and Lockett were released from Federal jail without having reported back by the expected time, Luther "Lute" Houston was specifically hired and deputized as an undercover agent to check on them and the activities at the Hughes ranch.

Lute's sister Mattie had been married to Jim Hughes, but that marriage had ended in a very bitter divorce. Lute was not involved in their marital problems and had remained on reasonably friendly terms with Jim. Lute lived in Chickasha, as did several members of his well-respected family.

Houston was recruited by Chris Madsen and hired as a deputy U.S. marshal to go to work for his former brother-in-law and report to the authorities on the activities at the Hughes ranch. Houston had prepared one message at Mountain View to be sent to Deputy Marshal Chris Madsen at Chickasha. Smith Brown, a hack driver, was lounging around the telegraph station and saw the name of the sender and the addressee. He knew the Hughes brothers and never wasted any time in informing them that their employee had contacted an officer.[1]

The U.S. marshal's office remained silent about Lute Houston when Casey and Sims were killed, even though an unidentified body had been found near Swan Lake, and they soon realized that their third special deputy assigned to the case was unaccounted for. On October 29, 1902 (five days before Bert Casey and Jim Sims were killed at Cleo Springs), the body of an unknown man had been found in the Eakly neighborhood. The body had been discovered by J.W. McElroy, a farmer in the community.

"The body when found was lying in a thicket on the banks of Cobb creek and to all appearances had lain there for about two weeks. It was lying face down, with the hands tied behind his back and a rope about his neck. A long coil of the rope lay beside the body, which evidently had been dragged some distance. The body was that of a rather small and comparatively young man with dark brown hair. The face was in such advanced stage of decomposition as to be unrecognizable, even had it been seen by those who knew him in life. A slicker was found on the body and black socks were on his feet, but no shoes. One foot was partly torn away, supposed to have been eaten by coyotes. It was presumed that the murdered man had met his death in connection with stealing horses. The authorities were notified of the discovery."[2]

The body was later identified from his cuff buttons and clothes by his mother as being that of her son Lute Houston. It was determined that he had been hanged to a nearby limb, also shot, then dragged about thirty yards into the brush. His boots had been removed, and one foot had been partly eaten off. An inquest was held, and the jury found that he had come to his death at the hands of parties unknown.[3]

Upon closer examination his boots were found, as was the very tree upon which he had been hanged. Also, it was determined that not only had he been hanged and shot through the chest, but his slayers had crushed his skull over his left ear.[4]

Because of the many recent crimes of Bert Casey in Caddo County, his name was soon related to the lynching of Deputy

Marshal Lute Houston. The Hughes brothers then became suspects, due to their association with Casey and the proximity of their ranch, which was located only six miles west of the crime site.[5]

Ben and Jim Hughes were called to Cordell, which had recently garnered the county seat from Cloud Chief, to answer some sundry charges. Their responses were satisfactory, and they were released. "Before they could leave the courthouse they were arrested by a Deputy U.S. Marshal and Caddo County Sheriff Jim Thompson. They offered bond, which was refused and the night found them sheltered in the Cordell jail. The following morning they were taken to Anadarko, to be tried in the county where the crime [murder] was committed."[6]

After the inquest, the body (of Houston) had been wrapped in a sheet and buried where it was found, near Swan Lake. It had later been exhumed for further examination and confirmation of identification. The preliminary trial of Jim and Ben Hughes was held in Anadarko, by Judge Starkweather, on April 19, 1903.

The first witness was J.W. McElroy, who testified that he and a neighbor had found the body. His statements as to the location and condition of the body were compatible with the previous reports. Sam Huddleston, the neighbor who had been with McElroy when they discovered the body, was the second witness called. His testimony was substantially the same as that of the first witness.

> The third witness, Mrs. Mattie R. Smith, of Chickasha, testified that the late Lute Houston was her brother, that he was about 35 years old, and unmarried. That he had been employed near Mountain View, to which place he had gone to locate someone, presumably Bert Casey, for the officers. Witness was present when the body of the murdered man was exhumed, and positively identified the clothing as that worn by her brother, when she last saw him, some time during the latter part of September. Was positive in her identification of the articles, especially the

boots, were not on the corpse, but had been found after the body was discovered. Witness testified that Jim Hughes, one of the defendants, was her first husband, and the father of her son James F. Hughes. The voice of the witness trembled and she displayed considerable feeling when describing the appearance of the corpse. She testified that the corpse of the skull showed evidence of the three blows of sufficient force to crush the skull.

The fourth witness, James F. Hughes, familiarly known as "Wizzer" testified that he was the son of Jim Hughes, and nephew of the late Lute Houston; that on the last day he saw his uncle Lute alive (Oct. 20, 1902) he kissed him goodbye and told him he never expected to see him again. Said he felt sure that his uncle was to be killed, but did not connect his father or Ben Hughes with the commission of the crime. Said that Bert Casey had threatened to shoot witness. Casey suspected witness of being in collusion with others to deliver Casey to the officers, as Smith Brown had so informed him. Witness testified that he had had trouble with his father, and seemed to have no hesitancy in testifying against his father. Testified that he knew both Hudson and Casey.

The fifth witness was Fred Hudson the man who shot Bert Casey, the noted outlaw. Witness testified that on October 20, he was at the Hughes ranch on the Washita river north of Mountain View. That he saw Jim Hughes, Bert Casey and Will Crossland. That Casey referred to Crossland as his best friend. Witness testified that he and Casey had been together since October 9, that they had met on Rainy Mountain creek, also that he was a deputy U.S. marshal, at the time he, Casey and Sims were hiding at Stone's canyon.[7]

Judge Starkweather ruled that there was not sufficient evidence presented to hold Ben Hughes, and he was released. Jim Hughes and Will Crossland, a neighbor, were held over. The trial attendants were so outspoken in asserting that the Hughes brothers should be hanged that the judge granted a change of venue for the future trial. Bert Casey's name also appeared on the docket, which served only to document the case, as he had been killed five days after Houston's body was discovered.

A few days later, a hearing was held to determine if Crossland should be bound over for trial. It was determined that he was not involved in the murder, and charges against him were dropped. Later, murder charges were filed against Ben Hughes and Fred Hudson. Three years passed before the Hughes brothers and Fred Hudson were tried for the murder of Lute Houston. Their trials will be covered in a later chapter.

After Houston's body was exhumed, it was placed in a coffin and released to Mrs. Smith and John Houston, then was taken to Chickasha for burial.[8]

CHAPTER 19

Territorial Courts and Trials

The trial of Pete Williams, who had been with Bert Casey when Sheriff Smith and Deputy Beck were killed, was held at Anadarko. He was charged with "complicity in the murder," and tried in July 1902. Williams was found guilty and was sentenced to ten years in the penitentiary.[1]

Joe Mobley, the other young man who was with Bert Casey when the two lawmen were killed near Anadarko in January 1902, was granted a change of venue. His trial was held in Hobart, in September 1903. Joe's mother had prevailed upon Moman Pruiett, a young attorney at Pauls Valley who was gaining a reputation for getting his clients acquitted, to defend her son. Nonetheless, Mobley was convicted and sentenced to five years imprisonment.[2]

Years later, attorney Pruiett related that Mobley's mother was in dire circumstance, but he had taken the case and had paid all of the expenses out of his pocket. When he was asked why the jury had given Mobley only a five-year sentence when Pete Williams' sentence had been twice that long, Moman responded, "We just made a good show out of it. I made 'em think about Joe's poor mother, instead of the dead lawmen. They were feelin' right sorry for Joe's maw before we got through."[3]

The court session that was to hear the cases of Mort Perkins and George Moran, charged with the murder of Jay Beemblossom, opened on October 30, 1902. The prisoners had been in jail at Guthrie, then transferred to Lawton for their trials.

There had been speculation that Bert Casey would lead a gang of gunmen into Lawton to free his former cohorts. Numerous rumors had spread that an attack by the Casey gang was imminent. Officers at Lawton were on the alert. One such occasion was reported: "Bert Casey the outlaw, appeared in Lawton last Sunday and his presence was reported to the local officers, who began searching for him. Casey lost no time in leaving town. Heck Thomas lost a valuable gun while looking for Casey."[4]

One of the later newspaper accounts of Hudson and Lockett's killing of Casey and Sims reported: "Had the Cleo Springs scheme failed, the outlaws were to be led into a trap by attempting to liberate their partners, Moran and Perkins, now in jail at Lawton, and on trial for murder."[5] Whatever hope that Moran and Perkins may have entertained that Casey was going to rescue them from the officers vanished shortly after Moran's trial started, when word was received at Lawton that Casey and Sims had been killed at Cleo Springs.

The 1902 fall session of court in Comanche County was held in a church at Lawton, because a courthouse had not yet been erected. Judge Frank Gillette presided over the trial of George Moran. One of the attorneys for Moran was John Jennings, who had been wounded in the gunfight with Temple Houston at Woodward a few years earlier.[6]

"Quanah Parker [Chief of the Comanches] was disqualified from serving on the jury in the Moran murder case on account of his imperfect knowledge of English. The attorneys for the defense sailed right into Quanah right and left, saying that he was a polygamist and not an American citizen."[7]

"George Stone [the deputy sheriff] who was shot through the thigh at the time that Walter Swofford was killed and Mort Perkins was captured, in Seminole Nation, was in Lawton, for the trial. He is crippled for life."[8]

"Dr. Beemblossom, father of the murdered boy, was the first witness. He told the story of the holdup and murder, in a plain but graphic manner. Still when he came to relate how the boy, wounded unto death, lay in his arms and begged the bandits, not to kill papa, he was visibly shaken. Prof. Esly of the Tulsa Indian school, Mr. Milder and Harry Darbyshire, all of whom were present when the killing occurred, testified. They made a strong case against the prisoner."[9]

"The defense presented a livery man from Davis that testified that Moran, under the name of Brown traded horses with him the night before the robbery. A dairyman swore that he was present at the time of the trade, and brought the horse that Moran swapped off. Still another man swore that Moran [or Brown] had written a note [at Davis] the day of the murder. Since Davis is sixty miles from Rush Springs, the argument is that he [Moran] could not have been present at the hold-up."[10]

Both the prosecution and defense presented their sides of the case at length, then it went to the jury. After twenty-four hours they remained deadlocked on a verdict. The jury stood nine for conviction, and three for acquittal. Judge Gillette considered that a verdict could not be reached, declared a mistrial, and rescheduled the case for the next term of court.[11]

A few days later, the case against Mort Perkins for the murder of Jay Beemblossom followed the same course as had Moran's trial and likewise ended in a hung jury. The second trial for Mort Perkins was held at Lawton, in April 1903. He was convicted and sentenced to "life in prison."[12]

Immediately following Mort Perkins' second trial, the case against George Moran was tried, again. The result of Moran's second trial was the same as the Perkins' verdict. He too was convicted and sentenced to "life in prison."[13]

Young Jay Beemblossom had been murdered at a site that was within designated "Comanche County," but at the time that it occurred, Comanche had not been organized as a county. The defending attorneys thought that this technicality would be sufficient to gain relief from the lifetime sentences. In 1905 they filed habeas corpus proceedings on behalf of Moran, who was then confined along with Perkins in the penitentiary at Lansing, Kansas.[14]

The appeal was denied in December 1906 by the Court of Appeals at St. Louis. The attorneys planned to proceed with the appeal to the Supreme Court of the United States.[15] The Federal Supreme Court did not overturn the decision.

After serving about nine years of his sentence, George Moran was granted a parole. Less than a year later, Mort Perkins was likewise paroled. After release, each apparently lived within the law, as neither man was returned to prison to finish his sentence.

CHAPTER 20

The Defense of Tom Powell

While Bert Casey was still at large, robbing people, stealing horses, eluding and killing lawmen, Tom Powell, his partner in the murder of Rufus Choat, remained in jail awaiting trial. Powell had been moved to the jail at Pauls Valley where his trial was held in early December 1901. The local newspaper briefly described the case as follows:

"Tom Powell and Bert Casey, who kept a saloon across the river in Oklahoma at Young's Crossing, waylaid and killed a man named Choat, under the impression that they were killing a man named Oxley, who had been flashing a roll of money in the 'Box' saloon. It seems that Oxley was warned by a friend who had taken him home by a different route, and a penniless man, who was a friend of the prisoner [Powell] became the victim."[1]

Moman Pruiett, who had become a much-in-demand attorney for the defense, lived in Pauls Valley and was approached by Nora Powell, Tom's sister. Nora, who was an attractive young school teacher, offered him her total savings and pleaded with him to defend her brother. The evidence against Powell was very strong and logically was undeniable. Nora eagerly offered that she would help Moman in any way she could be of service. Her personal appeal to the popular attorney was very persuasive.

Pruiett reluctantly agreed to represent her brother Tom.

Powell's first trial ended when the jury could not reach a decision. The judge declared a mistrial and rescheduled the case for the next court session.

Nora's hope and Pruiett's goal was to obtain an acquittal for his client. Moman tried to plot a defense that would triumph over the much-witnessed evidence. Pruiett's defense of Powell at his second trial was one of his many unusual cases. The attorney's version of the defense which he arranged for Powell is recorded in his life story titled *Moman Pruiett, Criminal Lawyer.*[2]

This was an extremely stressful period in Pruiett's hectic personal life. Not only was he constantly travelling throughout the Territories and Texas presenting the defense of his many clients, but while Powell lingered in jail, Moman's wife became ill and died. His frequent returns to his home base of Pauls Valley enabled Moman to maintain frequent contact with Nora and communicate with his client.

The slothful Tom Powell was afflicted with a ponderous pair of flat feet, which flapped inward. When the men from "The Box" saloon had arrived at the site of the murder, Choat was found dead and his pockets empty. Their lanterns had plainly revealed tracks around the body, imprinted by one with huge shoes and a pigeon-toed stride, leading across the moist sand to the river bank.

Nora was helpful in Moman's turbulent life and his preparation for the upcoming case. Following the guidance of Pruiett, she coached her indolent brother to walk with his toes pointing outward. This was essential for his planned defense. Pruiett was able to delay Tom's trial from one session to the next. Not only did these delays grant Nora additional time to accomplish her simple but extremely difficult task of teaching her benighted brother, but they made it more likely that the prosecutor would not be able to produce as many of the numerous witnesses to Tom's telltale tracks at the murder site.

For his, as well as his client's, benefit, Pruiett stalled Tom's second trial for three years. In mid-November 1904 the defense was ready, and Powell's case was called again. Bail had recently been arranged for the prisoner. Moman had Tom and Nora in his office for daily rehearsals the last few days, to insure that his bumbling client performed appropriately at his trial.

As the case unfurled, the defense met the prosecuting attorney's brigade of witnesses head-on. For every one of the state's witnesses to swear that they knew Tom Powell and that he walked noticeably pigeon-toed, the defense produced two witnesses who testified to the contrary. Moman provided a good alibi for Powell. Pruiett sensed that the defense was looking good when he whispered to Tom, "Remember, keep those damn toes turned out," and put Powell on the witness stand.

After Powell's attorney asked his client some routine questions to put Tom at ease, Moman proceeded by stating:

"Now Tommy, certain people who don't know you very well have intimated that you are pigeon-toed. Are you?"

"Naw, sir," answered Tom.

"Have you ever walked with a pigeon-toed gait, that is, with your toes turned, like this?" The attorney demonstrated his meaning.

"Naw, sir," Tom answered.

"Tommy, I want you to take your shoes and stockings off."

Moman waited as the awkward youth twisted in the witness chair, removing his large heavy shoes and coarse socks.

"Now, son," he said. "I want you to walk down here to where I am, an' remember to walk in your most natural way. I mean, the way you walked when you took your first steps, hanging to the hem of your mother's apron, an' as you've walked naturally, to this good day."

The direct request was too strong for dim-witted Tom; it had been formulated by the defense to convey a strong message and display to the jury that his client walked in a normal manner. Powell pondered for a moment, then followed the directions, literally. "He stepped down with his big feet toed-in and walked toward his lawyer, with his toe nails raking the ankle of the opposite foot each languid stride."

The resourceful Moman Pruiett stood silent, as he could

think of nothing to attempt a cover-up of the demonstration that so abruptly and absolutely shattered his long-planned and much-practiced defense. The prosecutor sat smugly at his table and, when asked, with a grin confidently replied, "No cross-examination."[3]

The jury found Powell guilty and sentenced him to "life in prison."[4] Nora was relieved that it was not the death penalty, while Pruiett responded, "That's the first case I ever lost an' was damn glad of it."

The life sentence imposed on Tom Powell for his role in the murder of Rufus Choat was one of the most severe punishments ever pronounced against one of Pruiett's clients. Whether it was ever appealed or altered is not known. Moman had no inclination to seek relief, as he had been humiliated and had no tolerance for anyone unable or unwilling to grasp any possible means by which to escape punishment of the law.

CHAPTER 21

Moman Pruiett,
Attorney for the Defense

Moman Pruiett, who had defended Joe Mobley and Tom Powell in their respective murder trials in which each had been an accomplice of Bert Casey, went on to become one of the most successful defense attorneys in the United States. He came into Indian Territory in 1895 and resided in Oklahoma the remainder of his life except for a short time he lived in Florida. Pruiett practiced law throughout the South and Southwest. Since Pruiett cast a dark shadow over the Twin Territories, and for many years after statehood, some of the highlights of his stormy personal life during his controversial career will be outlined.

Moman was the son of Warren L. and Elizabeth (Moorman) Pruiett. He was born on July 12, 1872, at Alton, Illinois.[1] His given name was a contraction of his mother's maiden name. Warren had served in the Confederate army during the Civil War, and was afterward called "Captain" by his friends. The Pruiett children were raised amid Southern attitudes and traditions. Moman was very individualistic, and his entire life was one of turmoil and controversy. He was constantly at odds with society, as his temper and ironfisted nature led him from one conflict to another.

Moman's antisocial attitude surfaced early in life and caused him trouble in school at Hackett City, Arkansas. He refused to conform to the norm and was not well accepted by the other students. He fought all of the boys in school and within a few months was fighting with the teachers. These tantrums precluded his obtaining but little formal education.[2]

At sixteen (in December 1887), Moman was convicted of forgery and was sentenced to two years in the state penitentiary at Little Rock.[3] He was pardoned in 1888, after serving eight months of the sentence. Upon his release the Pruiett family moved to Paris, Texas. Moman then got a job cleaning the office of attorney Jake Hodges, where he also started "readin' law."

Two years after being convicted in Arkansas, he was charged with a robbery at Paris and was again convicted. He was sentenced to five years in the state penitentiary at Rusk, Texas. Immediately after the sentence was pronounced, Moman shook his clenched fist at the jury and vowed a vengeance against society, shouting: "You'll regret this, every damned one of you. I'll empty your jails and turn thieves and murderers loose on you—and I'll do it in a legal way."[4]

Moman was paroled after serving two years of the sentence. Upon his release, he returned to Paris and worked at the only job that the twice-convicted felon could get. Fortunately, the young man was exceptionally strong, as his new employment was "tussling" bales of cotton in a warehouse. After the work day at the warehouse, he would clean the attorney's office in the evening, then study law for hours. With no formal training and only a little help from Jake Hodges, but lots of determination, Moman Pruiett was admitted to the Texas bar at the age of twenty-three.[5]

A few months later he moved to Pauls Valley, in the Chickasaw Nation, where he "hung out his shingle." Pruiett was soon practicing law in Indian and Oklahoma Territories, then commonly known as the Twin Territories.

Moman continued to study law diligently and learned to practice law ruthlessly. His avowed vengeance, which had been considered only an outburst of teenage temperament, was soon recognized as his true life's goal. He obtained acquittals by resorting to any means at hand, with no regard to any element of ethical standards. If he thought he "could pull it off and get by with it," he culled no means to gain freedom for a client. His disdain of the law enabled him to present fraudulent testimony and evidence in behalf of his clients with great pride and no penitence.

His methods proved to be very beneficial for his clients, as he usually swayed the jury to bring back a not-guilty verdict. Pruiett's courtroom shenanigans were praised by his clients, but they often irritated opposing lawyers, local law-abiding citizens, and frequently the judges. Anyone who expressed any indignation at his performance was challenged to fight, an exercise which he considered routine, necessary, and even enjoyable. Moman had lots of opportunities throughout his life to practice his expertise at fisticuffs and was always ready for another. His personal conflicts and encounters with the law are numerous. Some are described here to demonstrate the volatile disposition and disreputable character of this very successful attorney.

In May 1899, Moman pistol-whipped fellow attorney, T.N. Robnett, for interfering with the city marshal's arrest of Robnett's client. Pruiett was Pauls Valley's city attorney and accompanied the marshal to make the arrest. When Robnett attempted to delay and interfere in the marshal's mission, Pruiett struck Robnett with his six-shooter.[6]

During the winter of 1902, Pruiett shot and wounded Charley Wiseman (a drunken drifter who was a friend of Moman's brother, White, and who hung out at the Pruiett home) for wearing Warren's (Moman's father's) new coat. Moman shot Wiseman in each arm, and he fell into a muddy street in Paul's Valley. When Charley managed to get to his feet, he started to run but a third shot hit him in the leg.

Wiseman was irate and expressed to the doctor who was treating him his intention to see that the law would teach Moman a lesson. The doctor advised him that Moman had been charged with assault numerous times, but that the cases had all been dropped. The medic suggested to Wiseman that if he really wanted to be sure that Moman was held accountable for his act, he should lie down and die, then the charge would be murder, and surely Moman would be tried. Wiseman let the doctor know that he was not that mad and if the doctor could just fix him up so he could leave town, he would do so. The doctor did his job well, and Wiseman saw fit to move on. The charges against Pruiett were dropped shortly after Wiseman left the country.[7]

Pruiett was staying at the Byrd Hotel, in October 1903, while one of his cases was being tried in Ada, I.T. (Indian Territory). Dr. Thredkill of Allen, a small town near Ada, entered the hotel and demanded a room, and a woman. The proprietor tried to put the doctor out of his place of business and called upon Moman for assistance. Thredkill drew a pistol, and Pruiett shot him in the stomach, as the doctor's weapon failed to fire. After Thredkill sobered up, he admitted total fault. The doctor recovered from his wound, and Moman was exonerated.[8]

While waiting for the jury to reach a verdict in a murder case at Pauls Valley in December 1904, Moman and his client, Dr. F.B. Tyree, passed the time by swigging "the demon rum." Pruiett had previously defended Tyree and had gotten him acquitted of an earlier murder charge. Tyree thought that Moman had failed to present his second case in the best light and expressed that opinion in rather strong terms. As the drinking continued, Tyree's emotions became physical, and he threw a whiskey bottle at his attorney. Moman then hit Tyree over the head with another whiskey bottle. A druggist finished tending Tyree's cuts just in time for Pruiett to lead his head-bandaged client into the courtroom, as the jury returned and announced their verdict—"not guilty."[9]

While Pruiett was involved in a case in Kansas City, Pauls Valley attorney L.C. Andrews sent a message to the opposing counsel which was derogatory of Pruiett's character. When Moman returned to Pauls Valley, he pistol-whipped Andrews. Pruiett was tried for assault and found not guilty. At the mayor's insistence the controversial attorney was tried on a second charge for the same offense, this time for carrying a concealed weapon. Again the verdict was not guilty.[10]

Pruiett was a delegate to the Oklahoma constitutional convention held in Guthrie. He was prominent and outspoken on the many issues. One county was to be named "Moman," in his honor. The well-known attorney from Pauls Valley was planning to run for the state senate in the upcoming first election. Moman backed the wrong man in the power struggle for leadership. The opposition came through with the big votes at the convention, and Pruiett's man lost his dominating role. What had been intended to become Moman County then became Creek County. The Pauls Valley attorney had lost his political clout. The night that the convention adjourned, Pruiett and another delegate, an attorney by the name of Henshaw, got into a fight in the bar of Guthrie's Royal Hotel, where both were staying.[11]

By this time, Pruiett was being referred to as the lawyer with "the raving voice and raven hair" (he had exceedingly thick, black hair). Some referred to him as "the dark horse of the Washita." He had gained his reputation as a brawler shortly after he arrived in Pauls Valley, by whipping several of the local toughs.

Moman had defended many clients charged with "larceny of horses" in the Territorial courts. He was so successful in pleading their cases with his heart-rending appeals and fraudulent testimonies that at one time the Anti-Horse Thief Association seriously considered hanging him.

Once, Bert Casey went to Pauls Valley and consulted with Pruiett about what the miracle-working attorney might be able to do to beat the numerous charges of murder and larceny that were pending against the young outlaw.[12]

Pruiett's name became sacred among the criminal element. In many cases he made a farce of the judicial system, which he appeared to hold in contempt. He also seemed to delight in the agitation shown by local citizens at some of the not-guilty verdicts awarded to his clients.

Moman's consistent record of winning his cases enabled him to set his fee at any figure he happened to feel the urge to demand. Typically, he considered the person's ability to pay, the evidence of the case, and his own degree of personal interest. In some cases, he took everything that wealthy men had, in exchange for the freedom that he could almost guarantee them. Frequently, a farmer would drop off a bale of cotton each fall in payment for services rendered years before. This became such a popular means of remuneration at Pauls Valley that Moman arranged to warehouse this valuable commodity until the market was favorable.

About the time that Oklahoma gained statehood (1907) and Prohibition became the law, Moman moved from Pauls Valley to Oklahoma City. Pruiett's triumphs in the courtroom had become so routine that his acceptance of a case instilled a foregone conclusion by the populace that the accused would be acquitted.

On one occasion, when the local citizens learned that Pruiett had been retained to defend four men (Jim Miller, B.B. Burwell, Jess West, and Joe Allen) who were charged with the murder of A.A. "Gus" Bobbitt, they broke into the Ada jail, removed the prisoners, and hanged them. The conflict that resulted in Bobbitt's murder, and the subsequent lynching of the four men, had started years before when Bobbitt, West, and Allen were partners and operated the Corner Saloon.[13]

In February 1909, Fred Cardwell, counsellor for Governor Charles Haskell, charged Pruiett with "assault." He alleged that while Todd Warden, a special officer of the state, was securing evidence relative to violations of the prohibitory laws, Pruiett had drawn a gun on him. The judge refused to accept the case since the charge had not been processed through the county attorney.[14]

While Moman was in conversation with client W.D. Edwards on an Oklahoma City street in September 1912, they noticed a photographer preparing to take a picture. They assumed that the picture would include them. The attorney and his client did not want their picture taken, so they ran off the annoying photographer who reported to the police that "Pruiett hit him on the ear, almost knocking him down, and called him a vile name." Moman was arrested and fined five dollars.[15]

In February 1914, Governor Lee Cruce instructed the state attorney general to lead a crackdown on the bootlegging and gambling places. Oklahoma County sheriff M.C. Binion welcomed the support and began at once to raid the known joints. The first night netted the arrest of more than a hundred men. Pruiett hurried to the jail to talk with some of his regular clients who had been caught in the raids. When Sheriff Binion told him that he would have to wait for the men to be processed before he would be permitted to visit them, Moman became irate. Pruiett threatened the sheriff, but had no gun. The sheriff hit the attorney a glancing blow on the shoulder. They were separated before either got into action.[16]

While returning from Fort Worth, Texas, in April 1918, Moman and former district judge W.M. Maben, of Shawnee, were removed from the train at Waurika and charged with "introducing liquor" into Oklahoma. There was considerable scuffling with the officers before the men were arrested and handcuffed. The deputies who arrested the two friends and officials in the legal profession reported that they took twelve quarts of whiskey from Pruiett and six from Maben. A gun was removed from each prisoner. When the case came up, Pruiett pleaded guilty and paid the fine.[17]

Oklahoma County officers had cause to search Moman's car in September 1920. They found evidence that it had been used to transport whiskey into the "dry state." The officers went to the attorney's home and searched, but found only one quart of liquor. Moman was arrested and made bond the next day. Disposition of the case is not known.[18]

In October 1921, Pruiett and two other men were at the home of Joe Patterson, in Oklahoma City. Patterson, a Negro, was a well-known bootlegger and gambler. An argument developed among the group. Threats were made, guns were drawn, then Patterson was shot and killed. Moman called the police, surrendered, and admitted killing the black man. He was held in jail overnight and released on bond the next morning.[19] The following day, a coroner's jury was held at the inquest. The jury issued a verdict that Pruiett had been justified in killing the gambling bootlegger.[20]

During the evening of the same day that the coroner's jury determined that Pruiett was not guilty of any wrongdoing in killing Joe Patterson, he got into another gun affray. Pruiett and Sam Clement were at the Kingkade Hotel in Oklahoma City when trouble developed between the two lawyers. Clement was a well-respected attorney who had no known animosity against Moman, but on that occasion he became riled, drew his pistol, and threatened to kill Pruiett. Moman grabbed Sam's pistol and got his finger between the cocked hammer and cylinder, then wrestled the weapon from Clement's grasp. The confrontation was broken up before further damage was done. Moman nursed a cut, badly bruised finger for a few days.[21]

In January 1922, Frank Eckerly accused Moman Pruiett of assaulting him with a gun. The victim tried to get Oklahoma County attorney Forrest Hughes to issue a warrant for the arrest of Pruiett. Hughes refused to do so unless Eckerly produced witnesses to the reported assault. Eckerly stated that he would appeal to the governor. No further information about the case has been found.[22]

Moman was ill several months during the first half of 1923. He spent much of the time in the Baylor Baptist Sanitarium, at Fort Worth. In July of that year he was arrested in that Texas city when officers found a quart of whiskey in his car. Also in his company were several of the nurses from the hospital. Moman advised the officers that they were celebrating his recent recovery. When charged, Pruiett pleaded not guilty and posted bond. Disposition of the case is not known.[23]

Pruiett was arrested, in September 1927, for loitering around McGaffery's place on East First Street, in Oklahoma City. The attorney claimed that he, with two ladies from Ponca City and a client from Seminole, had gone to the Negro bootlegger's place trying to locate a witness to the murder with which his client was charged. The controversial attorney acknowledged that while there, the four did have a drink. McGaffery's place was a popular "bootleg joint."

When the case was heard, McGaffery's attorney argued so fervently that he convinced Judge O.P. Estes that his Negro client never sold whiskey. The judge then logically reasoned that if Moman and his guest had a drink while at McGaffery's place, then he must have brought his own booze. The judge then changed the charge to "possession." Moman Pruiett, the celebrated criminal lawyer whose heart-rending appeals, conniving ways, and underhanded manipulation of evidence and witnesses had persuaded countless juries to acquit horse thieves, rapists, and murderers, was unable to convince the steadfast judge that his party had taken no whiskey to the "bootleg joint" but had simply purchased drinks at the popular oasis where they were arrested. Moman was dumbfounded, but paid the ten-dollar fine.[24]

Pruiett and two other attorneys were meeting in February 1934 when a disagreement surfaced. Moman claimed that C.D. Peck had struck him with a steel rod, before he drew his pistol. Attorney Peck claimed that Moman pulled his gun, then he hit Pruiett with the rod, just as the weapon fired. No one was seriously hurt, and the charges were dropped.[25]

In late February 1935, the Congress Club, owned by Moman Pruiett and operated by his son-in-law, was raided by Cleveland County officers. The club was located south of Oklahoma City, conveniently situated on the lee side of the Oklahoma County line. The officers found liquor and gambling equipment, and arrested more than fifty people. The building was padlocked. Charges were filed against Pruiett and several others. Disposition of the case is not known.[26]

In July 1935, the Oklahoma State Bar Association recommended that Moman Pruiett be disbarred. The case involved was headlined "A FAKE CITY LOVE BALM SUIT" by the local newspaper. The details of the affair (or affairs) were perhaps too off-color and involved a class of society which kept descriptive publication of the case very minimal. Only Pruiett's role in the legal aspects gained much publicity. Pruiett's lack of professional ethics was charged, not his personal misconduct. The case went to the Oklahoma State Supreme Court, and Pruiett was suspended from the practice of law for one year.[27]

After the suspension, Pruiett returned to the courtroom, but his demeanor was not as flamboyant as before. Apparently, the suspension and old age had also mellowed his activities outside of the courtroom, as his personal conduct afterward seldom made the newspapers.

Moman Pruiett had learned and practiced ways to overcome the law and get juries to ignore all evidence against any of his clients, unless it was so inescapable as to be clearly seen by the absolutely blind and loudly heard by the totally deaf. During his career, Moman Pruiett defended 343 clients whose crimes were punishable with the death penalty. He won acquittals in 303 of those cases. None of his clients were executed. Only once was the death sentence pronounced, and Moman obtained presidential clemency for that client.

The record of his accomplishments in his unscrupulous professional career proves his success as an attorney for the defense. While he had not "emptied the jails" as he had threatened when a youth, he had certainly kept the prison population greatly reduced. This partial listing of his personal conflicts shows that during most of his life he needed his own lawyer and should, perhaps, have spent more of that time in prison himself.

A young associate attorney, Howard K. Berry, with the approval and cooperation of Moman, prepared a manuscript for a book about Pruiett's life. During World War II, while Howard was in the service of his country, Moman reviewed the manuscript that Barry had titled "He Made It Safe To Murder." Pruiett deleted about one-half of the document, retaining only the portion that reflected him in the better light. Pruiett had obviously squandered the exorbitant fees that he had frequently collected and was then without financial means. He resorted to his friend Ben Preston to provide the funds to have

Ben Preston, left; Moman Pruiett, right. Last picture taken of Moman Pruiett. (From the author's collection.)

the book privately published, without the knowledge of Howard Berry.

The book, retitled *Moman Pruiett, Criminal Lawyer,* was printed by the Harlow Publishing Company of Oklahoma City. When the book came off the press in November 1944, there were many comments about it being well named, as Moman was considered by most people to be both a "criminal" and a "lawyer." The book names no author on the title page and when cataloged is usually listed showing Moman Pruiett as the author. When young Berry learned that Moman had published his manuscript, he filed a lawsuit against the aged attorney.

This suit was still pending when Moman became ill of pneumonia and died on December 12, 1945, while in the Oklahoma General Hospital at Oklahoma City.[28] The seventy-three-year-old Pruiett was buried in the Sunny Lane cemetery, in southeastern Oklahoma City. One of the pallbearers at the funeral was Howard K. Berry.[29]

The young attorney ultimately won his case and the rights to the manuscript and book. References to the book *Moman Pruiett, Criminal Lawyer* seldom identify its author, Howard K. Berry. Today, a copy of the book in any of its three printings is hard to find and when found is costly to purchase.

CHAPTER 22

Wes Hudson:
Had Gun, Did Travel

Little was known about Fred Hudson in Oklahoma Territory when on November 3, 1902, he shot and killed Bert Casey at Cleo Springs. The fact that he had rid the Territory of its most notorious outlaw of the time was ample grounds for him to be considered a hero by most people. No one appreciated the exploits of Hudson and Lockett more than did the lawmen who had sought to bring in Casey, but had failed to nab the young outlaw. Hudson, though small in stature, had done a big man's job. He had earned the right to be a free man and to receive the reward and the acclaim of the Territory.

Fred Hudson received but one thousand dollars of the anticipated bounty. Only that portion of the reward offered by the governor was paid, the other reported amounts failed to materialize. He and Lockett left the Territory shortly after collecting the much reduced prize money. It was later reported that not long after Lockett moved on, he was killed near St. Louis, Missouri, while in a gunfight with officers.[1]

As soon as Hudson cleared up his affairs with the Territorial authorities, he returned to his family, who lived near Harrison, Arkansas. He had been born on March 25, 1878, on Crooked Creek, near that northwestern Arkansas town. His given name was William Wesley, and he had been called "Little Wes" by family and friends, while growing up. The name "Fred," which he had used in the Territory, was not recognized by those who knew him in Arkansas.

The Hudsons were one of the oldest and most respected families in Boone County, Arkansas. Wes' father, William Wiley, was a prominent county official, farmer, and stockman. The senior Hudson was well regarded throughout the area. Little Wes' mother, Martha Francis Eliza (Thompson), had died when he was seven years old, a month later a baby sister also died. Little Wes' father later married Louisa Ann Morrison, and they had ten children, which enlarged the Hudson family to sixteen. Thirteen of the children reached maturity.

When Little Wes was growing up, he was regarded as a pleasant, capable lad who was willing to work and share. While helping farm and tend his father's livestock, he rode horses extensively. The Hudsons and their neighbors would gather their cattle and drive them to market at Eureka Springs. Little Wes was very helpful around the place and at an early age became a expert rider. As a young man he developed a love for firearms, especially the pistol. He frequently practiced drawing the weapon quickly and shooting accurately. Little Wes was less than average in height and slight of built. By the time he drifted into Oklahoma Territory, about the turn of the century, he was an accomplished horseman and very adept at handling a revolver.[2]

Hudson's early activities in the Territory are not recorded. Likewise, it is not known when or why he began using the name "Fred" in lieu of "Little Wes." At some point after Hudson arrived in the Territory he took up with Bert Casey. Marshal Fossett was aware of their past association when he recruited Hudson to go after Casey.

The earliest news item about Hudson in the Territory was in late December 1901, when he was arrested by Deputy U.S. Marshal W.C. Graves. His name was listed as "Fred Hudson, alias Fred Huddleson," and he was charged with robbing the post office at Gipp, O.T., a small town eight miles northwest of Arapaho. The article stated, "He is identified as the man who has been in almost a dozen hold-ups in the new country. The authorities have positive evidence against the man and will surely convict him." He was taken to the Federal jail at Guthrie.[3] Eight months later, while an inmate awaiting trial, Hudson struck the deal with Marshal Fossett that gained him his release and sent him on the trail to "get Bert Casey."

When Hudson returned to Boone County after his adventures in the Territory, he not only had the limited reward money but also a recently acquired impulse for gambling and a taste for liquor. His main interest was no longer working and helping on the family farm. Little Wes began to spend more of his time in the saloons of the area.

Only four months after killing Bert Casey, while he was visiting the saloons at Jasper, in Newton County, Arkansas, twenty miles south of Harrison, Hudson shot and killed another man. During the day of February 3, 1903, he became intoxicated and created a disturbance. Jasper city marshal Allen called upon Deputy U.S. Marshal Jim Keys to assist him in arresting Little Wes. When Hudson saw the officers approach, he reached for his pistol, and Allen fired at the young man. Four shots were fired by Little Wes and two each by Keys and Allen. One of Little Wes' shots hit Keys in the bowels, and the deputy marshal died two days later. Hudson had been hit in the chest, but the ball struck a rib then followed it and did not penetrate deep.[4] Hudson was arrested and placed in the jail at Harrison, but escaped. He hid out with family friends before being recaptured.[5]

After being caught and arrested again, Little Wes was taken to the penitentiary for safe keeping. His attorneys requested that he be released on bond. Their request was denied, but the denial was appealed. The case went to the Arkansas Supreme Court which ruled that he could be released on a fifteen-thousand-dollar bond. The bond was met with twenty-seven thousand dollars of securities, and Hudson was released until the scheduled date for his trial.[6]

After his release he returned to Oklahoma Territory. In April 1903, he appeared as a witness at Anadarko, in the preliminary

"Little Wes" Hudson and his horse. (Courtesy of Fred Hudson, Harrison, Arkansas.)

hearing of Jim and Ben Hughes for the murder of Lute Houston. It was not known in the Territory that the witness had been charged with a murder in Arkansas and was at that time free on bond pending trial.

A change of venue had been granted Hudson for his trial on the charge of murdering Jim Keys. The trial was held in September 1903 at Marshall (forty miles southeast of Jasper), the county seat of Searcy County, Arkansas. Many fine points of the law and the evidence were argued extensively. After the jury had deliberated thirty-seven hours, they brought forth a not-guilty verdict. The newspaper article that reported the trial and verdict added, "The defendant is a young man, well and favorably known, with excellent family connections and friends."[7]

Less than a year after Little Wes was acquitted of murdering Deputy U.S. Marshal Jim Keys, he drew his trusty pistol again and killed yet another man. Henry Barchman became the third known victim of young Hudson in two years. This incident occurred at the State Line Saloon, near Forsythe, Missouri. The saloon was located four miles north of Omaha, Arkansas, just north of the state line, in Taney County, Missouri. The saloon had recently been established to accommodate the railroad crews who were blasting through the mountains, building the bridges, and laying the rails.[8]

There were various accounts but few details reported of the conflict that prompted Little Wes to pull his weapon and shoot Henry Barchman. Some reports were favorable to Little Wes, while others painted him to be a wanton killer. The end result of the affray was that Barchman, the bartender of the State Line Saloon, was dead, and numerous witnesses had seen Hudson fire the shots. Some confusion developed between the officers of Taney County, Missouri, and officers at Omaha, Arkansas, as to who was to arrest young Hudson. This delay permitted Little Wes an opportunity to escape from the authorities, which he anxiously used to his advantage.[9]

Hudson immediately left Boone County and went to Little Rock, where he joined the "sporting crowd" at the poker tables.

Little Wes greatly enjoyed the faster pace of the city, the saloons, and the gambling halls. Within a few weeks he became suspicious that the authorities had learned of his presence and that he was about to be picked up.

Young Hudson then departed Arkansas and went to Louisiana. He spent several months living in New Orleans, Shreveport, and Mer Rouge (in the northeastern corner of that state), where he married a young lady. While living in that locale, Little Wes got into still another shooting scrape and again killed a man. His most recent victim was a Negro. Later when Hudson was asked about the Louisiana incident, his comment reflected a typical attitude of the era, "It was only a nigger and didn't count that much."[10]

Little Wes and his bride left Louisiana shortly after the Negro was killed and went back to Little Rock. They took rooms at the Pacific Hotel using the name "J.W. Shaw and wife." He returned to his favorite saloons and participated heavily in the drinking and gambling. Little Rock police became aware that young Hudson, who was still wanted in Missouri for the murder of Henry Barchman, was again in their city.

Little Rock police chief J.J. Hawkins and Detective Tom Newland entered Mitchell's Saloon on June 21, 1905, and arrested Little Wes. "He submitted without protest and willingly accompanied the officers to police headquarters. He readily admitted to having killed three men: Bert Casey, Jim Keys and Henry Barchman. Hudson did not deny that he had killed others, but that three was enough for them to know about, at that time. He stated that he could offer no explanation of why he killed Barchman, the bartender." Hudson willingly agreed to return to Missouri and stand trial on the murder charge still pending against him in that state.[11]

Missouri officials took custody of Little Wes and delivered him to Taney County to be tried for the murder of Henry Barchman. Hudson was ably represented at his trial in Missouri by his uncle, "Judge" Hudgins, of Harrison. The defense presented by "the judge" won for Hudson a not-guilty verdict.[12]

After his acquittal, Little Wes moved to Perryville, Arkansas, where a few weeks later his wife became ill and died. Oklahoma authorities had learned the whereabouts of their "Fred" Hudson in June 1905, when Little Wes was arrested in Little Rock. Investigation into the murder of Deputy U.S. Marshal Lute Houston, who had been lynched while working undercover three years earlier, was still ongoing. Jim and Ben Hughes had been indicted in 1903 for the murder of Houston. Fred Hudson had also been implicated in that hanging and was wanted by the Territorial officials.

In December 1905, Arkansas authorities were requested to arrest Hudson, as he was wanted in Oklahoma Territory on a murder charge. Caddo County deputy sheriff James C. "Big Jim" Bourland was sent to Little Rock to assist in the arrest and return the wanted man to the Territory. Big Jim was a large man, and his descriptive sobriquet was most appropriate. While passing through Perry (railroad depot of Perryville), en route to the Arkansas capital, Big Jim saw Little Wes on the station platform. "Bourland obtained the services of Special Agent McIntosh of the Rock Island Railway, to help him arrest Hudson by a ruse. McIntosh approached Little Wes and extended his hand, which Hudson took, while Bourland slipped behind him and took a large gun, which he carried." Hudson was arrested, taken to Little Rock, and held in jail until the extradition request was processed. Bourland then returned Hudson to Oklahoma Territory to be tried for the murder of Lute Houston.[13]

Bourland delivered Hudson to the Caddo County jail at Anadarko to be held until his trial, which was scheduled for the next term of court, in May 1906. Sheriff Thompson's deputy, Big Jim, had been deputized as a U.S. marshal shortly before his assignment to return Hudson from Arkansas. Bourland had been instrumental in working up the cases against the Hughes brothers and Hudson.[14]

CHAPTER 23

Lute Houston's Murder Trials

Wes "Fred" Hudson's trial for his part in the murder of Lute Houston was held before Jim and Ben Hughes' trial on the same charge. Hudson was tried at Anadarko, during the first week in May 1906. Fred's uncle, "Judge" Hudgins of Harrison, Arkansas, came to Anadarko and assisted in the defense of his nephew.

Hudson's trial went smoothly and was of short duration. One newspaper reported: "The most sensational part of the trial was the testimony of the defendant. He told of being released from the federal jail at Guthrie and deputized to capture Bert Casey, 'dead or alive.' He [Hudson] told in detail the meeting of the Hughes brothers and Casey with Houston and of the murder, which he was compelled to be an unwilling witness. Then, he followed with a narrative of the killing of Casey near Cleo, in Woods County. After hearing the evidence the jury returned a 'not guilty' verdict."[1]

Upon Hudson's acquittal of the murder charge against him, he was bound over to be a witness for the prosecution, at the Hughes brothers' trial. The change in venue granted by Judge Starkweather at Anadarko in 1903 resulted in the trial of Jim and Ben Hughes for the murder of Lute Houston to be held at Hobart, the county seat of Kiowa County. The case came before the court in mid-May 1906.

The wives of Ben and Jim Hughes had hired O.J. Logan, an attorney from Lawton, to defend their husbands. The Hughes brothers had engaged the services of their old friend Al Jennings to represent them in the trial.

After being captured by Deputy U.S. Marshal Bud Ledbetter near Sam Baker's home in 1897, Jennings had been tried, convicted, and sentenced to life in prison for his train-robbing efforts. While in prison, he was able to get his sentence reduced and had been paroled in November 1902. Upon his return to Oklahoma Territory, Al had joined his brother John in a law partnership at Lawton. President Roosevelt later granted Jennings a full pardon.[2]

Years later, Attorney Logan reflected back on the trial and recalled that he had been unaware that Jennings was involved until after he had accepted the case. He explained that "he and Al conferred and reached agreement on which would take the lead in the various segments of the trial. This arrangement was satisfactory to all parties and worked without conflict."[3]

Hudson testified that at the time when Deputy Marshal Houston was hanged, he too was a deputy U.S. marshal and had been sent out specifically to "bring in Bert Casey." "He testified that he was present at the scene of the murder, because; to have done otherwise would have interfered with his plans to capture Casey and would have endangered his own life. He further stated that he had heard the Hughes boys and Casey agree that Houston was a spy and ought to be killed. That he tried to evade being a party to their planned action, but found no way to do so."

Hudson acknowledged that "he rode with Casey and they met Jim Hughes and Lute Houston [as Casey and Hughes had planned]. At that point [near Swan Lake] Casey and Hughes put a rope around Houston's neck, led him into the brush and hanged him. When they returned to the place where he [Hudson] was holding the horses, each had one of the dead man's boots."[4]

"A large part of the time was consumed by the defense in producing evidence to refute the testimony of Fred Hudson. Four witnesses swore that Bert Casey was at the John Dunn ranch in Day county, eighty miles away, at the time of the killing. Six witnesses testified that on the day of the killing, they saw Hudson and Houston together in Mountain View. This was in contradiction of Hudson's statement that he never saw Houston that day, until he was produced by Jim [Hughes] at the time and place of the hanging. Then followed a half dozen or more witnesses who testified that Jim Hughes was at the Shelly pasture, eighteen miles away at the time of the killing."[5]

John Dunn's Day County ranch was not far from the outlaw's camp on Dead Indian Creek where Sheriff Bullard and Deputy Cogburn had been killed. This claim by four witnesses that Bert Casey was known to have been a visitor in this area prompts greater suspicion that he might have been the murderer of the officers. John Dunn had witnessed the murder of the Roger Mills County lawmen four months before Houston had been hanged.

"Jennings' argument to the jury was very effective. He did not admit that he had been an outlaw, but he did state that he knew something about them. He told the jury that in the name of 'God and High Heaven' not to send the Hughes boys to the penitentiary, but if they were guilty to hang them and save them from the terrors of the penitentiary. Jennings himself was at one time under a life sentence. Jennings' plea for acquittal of the Hughes boys was a personal matter. From what he said to the jury one would believe that the Hughes brothers had befriended Jennings during his days of outlawry and he was now repaying them with his legal service."[6]

Years later, when Attorney Logan related about the case, he explained that he had insisted on seating the strongest jury available, pointing out that normally lawyers for the defense preferred a weak jury. According to his recollection, Hudson's testimony included his stating that Hughes and Casey had left their revolvers and rifles with him to forestall Houston getting hold of one of them, in the event of a struggle. After Casey and Hughes pulled Houston clear of the ground they took their weapons from Hudson, then, they riddled the swinging body with bullets. On cross-examination, Logan asked Hudson why he had not fired on the unarmed Casey and Hughes, whom he would have had a right to shoot under the circumstance. The alert jury that Logan had seated, was able to grasp the incongruity of his statement.[7]

Late in the evening of May 21, 1906, the jury returned to the Kiowa County courtroom and issued their verdict. They found the Hughes brothers not guilty of murdering Lute Houston. The court records of the trial are not available, having been destroyed by fire.[8]

Al Jennings later moved his law practice to Oklahoma City, where in 1912 he ran for Oklahoma County attorney. He failed to win that election. In 1913, *The Saturday Evening Post* serialized a story written by Al Jennings and Will Irwin titled "Beating Back," which Al claimed was a true account of his life. Bolstered by the publicity that he had gained from the magazine articles, he ran for governor of Oklahoma in 1914; again his campaign was a lost cause. *Beating Back* was published as a book by D. Appleton & Co. of New York in 1915. The experiences related in the book are garbled. Most of the events described in the story lack the name of the location and the date of the claimed occurrence. Little factual information can be obtained from *Beating Back*; however, it did provide Al with some recognition outside of Oklahoma.

About the time that the movie-making business began to flourish in Southern California, Al moved into that area. In the world of pretense, a pretender will find a home, and so it was with Jennings. Al succeeded in convincing the movie producers that he was a former big-time, gunfighting "horseback outlaw of the old west." His welcome in California as a consultant for Western movies greatly exceeded his reputation in Oklahoma as an attorney, a politician, or a train robber.

Al's arrival in the new movie capital soon prompted a film based upon his book to be produced. This production portrayed Jennings to be brave and brilliant, while the men who chased him were depicted as cowardly simpletons of the law.

While Jennings was serving his prison sentence, he had become acquainted with William Sidney Porter, a fellow inmate. After Porter was released from prison, he wrote several well-accepted books using the pen name "O. Henry" and became a very successful author. Al then elaborated about his previous confinement with the currently popular author. Jennings wrote a book titled *Through The Shadows With O. Henry,* which was published by the A.L. Burt Co. of New York in 1921.

Another movie titled *Al Jennings of Oklahoma* was produced in the late 1940s. Again it was based on Al's version of his outlaw career. Other than the names of the Jennings family members, there was little that could be relied upon as factual, or even resembling true events.[9]

Al Jennings found his "calling" in Hollywood, where he lived to the ripe old age of ninety-eight and died on December 26, 1961. His death certificate listed his occupation as "self-employed guest speaker."[10]

Anadarko railroad depot, circa 1910. (Courtesy of Oklahoma Historical Society.)

CHAPTER 24

Showdown
in an Anadarko Saloon

When "Fred" Hudson was released by the court as a witness in the trial of the Hughes brothers for the murder of Lute Houston, he left Hobart and went back to Anadarko. Shortly after arriving on Tuesday afternoon, May 22, 1906, in the town where he had recently been tried for and acquitted of murder, Hudson was arrested by Deputy Jim Bourland for carrying a gun. His pistol was retained by the justice of the peace, and Hudson posted bond for his appearance in court the following morning.

Deep animosity had developed between Hudson and Bourland, who was also running for Caddo County sheriff while serving as Caddo County deputy sheriff and deputy U.S. marshal. Several newspaper articles of the time reported that Big Jim had been in prison prior to "pinning on the badge." One article reported that he and Hudson had been involved together in a train robbery a few years earlier. Another item reported that "while on the witness stand in the recent Hughes trial, Bourland admitted that he had 'served time' in Texas."[1]

The reports of Bourland's outlaw past have not been confirmed, nor has any information of previous companionship between Hudson and Bourland been located. The fact that Big Jim recognized Hudson (at the Perry depot) as the deputy's train was passing through would indicate that he was at least well acquainted with Hudson's appearance. It may be assumed that whatever association that there may have been between Bourland and Hudson at an earlier time, it had not developed into an everlasting friendship.

There may have been ill feelings between the two before Bourland deceptively used another party in arresting Hudson at the Perry, Arkansas, depot. Bourland's being the officer who brought Hudson back to Oklahoma Territory to face the charge of murder in the Lute Houston case had undoubtedly added to the friction between the two men.

The resentment between Bourland and Hudson was whetted during the recent trials. Big Jim had worked incessantly in trying to assemble evidence that would convict the accused. He had put forth great effort and was a witness who showed a strong personal interest in the prosecution of Hudson and the Hughes brothers. Big Jim objected when Hudson was permitted to become a witness for the state in the case against the Hughes brothers. The deputy sheriff was very disappointed in the verdicts of the recent murder trials.[2]

After Bourland arrested Hudson upon his arrival in Anadarko and took his pistol, Fred Hudson obtained another. He then continued to celebrate his recent acquittal.

There are varying accounts of the following encounter, each differing in some detail from the others. All of the local articles related that Bourland was a good and brave officer who was well respected by the local citizens. Some of the earliest articles report that the showdown occurred in the street. Some accounts report that Bourland was in the saloon when Hudson arrived, others relate that Hudson was at the bar when Bourland entered. Most of the items report that Hudson drew and fired his .32-caliber pistol, and Bourland went into action with his new .45-caliber automatic hand gun. The following brief account appears to be a realistic summary of the gunfight's highlights:

Shortly after midnight, Deputy Bourland was notified that Hudson was drinking in a local bar and appeared to be armed.

Jim Bourland. (Courtesy of Oklahoma Historical Society.)

Big Jim arrived at the saloon a few minutes later and entered. The two adversaries saw each other at about the same time, and each reacted as if convinced that the other was intent upon killing him. There was no hesitation. Their mutual approach exhibited courage and determination on the part of each, neither spoke nor wavered. "When the two men met at the time of the shooting, there was no parleying, each began at once, the deadly work."[3] Each man drew and fired his pistol at the other until unable to do so, then mortally wounded, crumpled to the floor.

The showdown between Hudson, who was known as "Little Wes" in his home state of Arkansas, and "Big Jim" from Texas, occurred in the Robinson Saloon, at Anadarko, O.T., at about one o'clock on Wednesday morning, May 23, 1906. This gunfight that resulted in the death of these two diverse men, each of whom had stood on both sides of the law, is a classic example of the logo of the manufacturer of the arms that were used in this "duel to the death": "It matters not any man's size, a Colt in his hand will equalize."

Bourland was shot through the abdomen by the one shot that Hudson triggered off. Big Jim fired four shots, hitting Fred once in each leg and missing his target twice. The bone in Hudson's right leg was shattered, and his left leg sustained a serious flesh wound. Both men were taken to the local hospital. The doctors recommended amputation of Hudson's leg which had the splintered bone, but he rejected their advice for several hours. From Bourland's abdomen, surgeons removed about thirty inches of intestines that had been injured by the ball passing through his body.[4]

Bourland died that same evening. The I.O.O.F. (International Order of Odd Fellows) conducted his funeral service on Thursday morning, May 24, 1906. To accommodate the multitude of people that were expected to attend, the service was held in the local opera house. At that time, "It was the largest funeral ever held in Anadarko. The services were attended by U.S. Marshal Jack Abernathy and several members of his force from Guthrie. Officers from Lawton, Hobart and some of the surrounding towns also attended."[5]

Bourland was thirty-seven years old, unmarried, and lived with his elderly mother. It is assumed that he was buried at Anadarko, but his grave is not identifiable. There is no legible marker of the site, and the available cemetery records do not extend to that time period.[6]

Later, when Hudson agreed for the surgeons to remove his leg, they held some hope that he might recover. He realized and accepted the likelihood of his death without comment, but did express his gratitude for the certain knowledge that he had out-lived his nemesis, Big Jim. The doctors made every effort to pro-long his life, at least until the arrival of his father from Arkansas, but failed. Hudson died about midnight on Thursday May 24, 1906, at the age of twenty-eight.[7] William W. "Little Wes" (alias "Fred") Hudson's body was returned to his home state where he was buried in the Hudgins-Hudson family cemetery, near Har-rison, in Boone County, Arkansas.[8]

Ben Hughes related many years later that "when we heard the news that Bourland and Hudson had shot each other to death, we killed a calf, called in all the dugout boys, had a feast, got drunk and had a big time."[9]

CHAPTER 25

"Hookey" Miller, a Man to Reckon With

George Daniel Miller was born on December 13, 1861, in Dallas County, Texas. His parents, Stephen and Mary (Guest) were married in Parker County, Texas, in 1857. Not much is known of George's youth except that he did obtain a third-grade education and developed a deep appreciation for fine horses. When he became a teenager he left home and started working on the range for one of the large cattle ranches. During the next several years young George worked for various spreads in Texas and made some of the cattle drives across Indian Territory to the Kansas cow towns. A month before his twentieth birthday, George joined the Texas Rangers. After serving six months under Capt. George Baylor, he was honorably discharged from the Rangers in May 1882. In 1885, George Miller married Nellie Mae Gibson. They had two children, Edward ("Ed"), born in 1886, and George Jr., born in 1889.[1]

George Miller left Texas and moved to Oklahoma Territory, but neither the date nor the reason for his move is currently known. It has been written that he left Texas to escape law officers who were on his trail for some crime, usually reported to have been the larceny of cattle or horses. No specific charge pending against him in Texas at the time of his departure has been confirmed. It does seem logical that he was "a wanted man" (or at least he believed himself to be) in that state, which might explain why a thirty-five-year-old husband and father would leave his wife with two sons and come to the Territory, then take up with a cutthroat outlaw. It is thought that Miller came to the Territory in the spring of 1895 and sometime later joined up with George "Red Buck" Weightman.

Weightman is reported to have been one of the most bloodthirsty desperadoes who ever plagued the Twin Territories. He was an experienced horse thief and had been convicted of the crime. Red Buck escaped from the officers while en route to prison, before joining the Doolin gang. Due to his ruthless nature he was run out of that gang by its leader, Bill Doolin. After being cast out of that outlaw band, he moved on and was practicing his chosen profession of looting and killing in what is now the western part of Oklahoma, at the time that George Miller arrived in that area from Texas.

Numerous crimes committed during the period in that area were thought to be the work of Red Buck, and in most cases there was one or more men with him. Miller and Weightman were reported to have spent some time while hiding from the law, at the Hughes ranch on the Washita. It is quite likely that George Miller and the Hughes brothers had been acquainted when the three lived in Texas.

There have been various accounts related about when George Miller and Red Buck Weightman met and how their association came about. One story is that they first met at Dolph Picklesimer's homestead where they engaged in a brief private conversation and soon thereafter rode off together. Another account reports that Miller, who was living with W.W. Glover, killed two of a neighbor's cows that had broken into their field and were eating the crop. He then left his friend's home to escape answering to the law for killing the cows and met Weightman while on the "owl hoot trail."

When Miller took up with Red Buck is not currently known. The crimes with which Weightman and his henchmen were accused and in which Miller may have been involved cannot be clarified at this time. There has been speculation that George

Miller may have been the man referred to at the time as "Charley Smith" who was running with Red Buck in the fall of 1895. Gus Holland was killed and his cattle stolen on Cheyenne Creek in Dewey County, early in September 1895. Red Buck and the mysterious "Charley Smith" were suspects of the crime. A few days later, Weightman and an ally joined with Joe Beckham and Elmer "Kid" Lewis and held up a train near Curtis in Woodward County, then the four got away.[2]

Deputy U.S. Marshal Chris Madsen was with a posse of Texas Rangers when on December 31, 1895, they located Red Buck Weightman, George Miller, and Joe Beckham holed up in "Comanche Country." In the gunfight that followed, Beckham was killed and Red Buck was wounded in the shoulder but escaped along with George Miller. Later, Miller acknowledged his part in that engagement.[3]

Miller and Weightman were together when W.W. Glover was killed at his homestead on Barnitz Creek about five miles west of Arapaho, on February 14, 1896. The outlaws had sent Glover, who was a friend of Miller's, to town to buy ammunition and supplies. While in Arapaho, Glover tipped off a lawman. Custer County undersheriff Montgomery with five deputies went to Glover's farm and secreted themselves in a crib behind a haystack. Glover then headed for the nearby canyon where the outlaws were hiding and led them into the trap. The posse "jumped the gun," which alerted the outlaws of their presence. The outlaw pair commenced firing at the hidden posse and their host. As Glover ran for cover he was hit by one of their shots and died moments later. The two outlaws, who were first thought to be George Miller and Jim Harbolt but were later identified as Miller and Weightman, escaped amid the flying bullets from the posse's rifles.[4]

Contemporary newspaper articles about Glover having been murdered spoke of him as only a hard-working farmer. Years later, the local newspaper of the area published an article pointing out that Glover had done some killing of his own, in his native state, before homesteading on Barnitz Creek. Prior to his coming to Oklahoma Territory, the murdered man had lived in Palo Pinto County, Texas. Perhaps, Miller and Glover had known each other long before they met in Custer County.[5]

Upon learning that a homesteader had been murdered near Arapaho, posses took to the field in search of the two outlaws. A few days later, Weightman and Miller were seen hiding along the Canadian River, some thirty miles northeast of Arapaho. They eluded the officers and headed south, with the posse on their trail. When the outlaws reached the Wichita Mountains, they separated and each looped around, then started back toward Custer County.[6]

The posse located the two at the homestead of Dolph Picklesimer on Oak Creek (five miles north of Canute). When Miller and Picklesimer emerged from the farmer's half-dugout on the morning of March 5, 1896, the posse was in place. The officers called for them to surrender, but Miller went for his gun and started firing toward the hidden deputies. One of the lawmen's first shots hit Miller's hand and knocked the weapon from his grasp; he then ran toward the shelter. Weightman appeared from the entryway and commenced shooting at the officers. He was gunned down and lay lifeless as Miller retreated into the dugout.

The officers waited until they heard Miller calling out "to come help him as he was shot all to pieces." Reluctantly, they then entered the earthen home and found Miller with his right hand mangled, having been virtually shot off by one of the posse's bullets. The tips of three fingers of his left hand had also been shot off. Deputy Sheriff Joe Ventioner had been seriously wounded by a slug that entered his abdomen and passed out his back.

The posse delivered the body of Red Buck Weightman and the two severely wounded men to Arapaho, the county seat. Deputy Ventioner's wound was tended by Dr. Williams, who reported that he considered the wound to be serious but not fatal. That evening, Miller's right hand was amputated, and the three injured fingers of his left hand were cropped and treated.[7]

A grand jury was convened at Arapaho in early April, and its members indicted Miller for the murder of W.W. Glover. His bond was set at seven thousand dollars. Being unable to raise bail, Miller was retained in jail. In mid-April 1896, he was transferred to the El Reno jail for safe keeping.[8]

Miller's bond was reduced to fifteen hundred dollars in October 1896. It is presumed that he posted bond and was released from jail until his trial date. Proceedings of the case and events of George Miller's life immediately following the date that his bond was reduced cannot be determined at this time. No record of Miller's being tried in the Territory for the murder of W.W. Glover has been located.[9]

The next documented account of George Miller is eight months later when he was sent to prison in Texas after being convicted in Haskell County for "the theft of cattle." He entered the Texas prison system on June 27, 1897, as Number 15437. While in prison, he was fitted with a steel hook on his right wrist, and inherited the moniker by which he would be known for the remainder of his life. After serving forty-two months of his four-year sentence, he was released on December 27, 1900, as George "Hookey" Miller.[10]

Following his release from prison, Hookey and his family lived near Matador, Texas. The year of 1901 was filled with much distress for Miller: his brother was killed in a farm accident, his mother died, and his wife was burned to death. The details of his wife's fiery death are not known.

In spite of his rough life of recent years, George Miller was not just a resentful, gun-toter who was looking for trouble; he was also a man of kindness and sympathy. A letter written sixty years after an incident tells of Hookey's personal sacrifice in befriending a destitute family and saving the man's life, while living near Matador. It also stated "that he was a fellow who was that way [kindhearted] until someone tried to run over him. He was a brave man and one who would fight to the last ditch for or against anything that he thought was right or wrong." Sometime after his wife's death, Hookey left Texas and took his two sons to

George D. "Hookey" Miller Sr. (Courtesy of Helen Gaines, daughter of George D. Miller Jr.)

Custer City, O.T. At Custer City Hookey worked at the cotton gin, which his brother owned.[11]

The charge against Miller for the murder of W.W. Glover must have been resolved in some manner satisfactory to the authorities because six years after he had been indicted for that crime, the easily identifiable (one-handed) Miller was openly working at a cotton gin only ten miles from Arapaho. Upon completion of the 1903 ginning season, Hookey took a job as bartender at the Corner Saloon. He then sent his sons to live with their grandparents at Matador.

The Corner Saloon was located on the Canadian River, three miles downstream from Youngs Crossing at the southeastern tip of Pottawatomie County. At the time that Hookey worked at the bar it was owned by J.M. McCarty. The saloon was in Oklahoma Territory, but flourished primarily on the whiskey business from the Chickasaw Nation on the south, across the river, and the Seminole Nation, only a few feet away on the east.

The Corner Saloon is reported to have been the most notorious saloon that has ever operated in Oklahoma. Its patrons primarily consisted of heavy boozers from "The [Indian] Nations" and renegades from throughout the Twin Territories. A multitude of these undesirables, misfits, and "wanted men" congregated in that area along the river. Gunplay was frequent, and killings were of common occurrence in and around the saloon, which was the original and remained to be the major establishment in Corner, O.T.[12]

With only a steel hook for a right hand and an impeded left hand, undoubtedly Miller had difficulty in performing some of his bartending chores; however, that same handicap proved to be an advantage in certain of his tasks. Some of the troublesome customers soon found that "the hook" could also be a very effective tool. The somber barkeep, armed with this potentially lethal weapon that he had literally "at hand," became accepted as a man with whom it was unwise either to trifle or to scuffle with. Miller overcame his handicap in many ways. He developed a special skill in handling and shooting a pistol and rifle, using his right hook and the limited digits of his left hand.

While employed at the saloon, Hookey and a local grist mill owner by the name of Jasper R. Trout must have had some trouble that was still ongoing. During a flood of the Canadian River in October 1904, Hookey shot and seriously wounded Trout.

Newspaper articles reporting the incident provide but few details and offer no reason for the shooting. Hookey left some notes about the episode which indicate that Trout, with his rifle, was on the roof of his house to escape the high water and was taking aim at Hookey, who was in water up to his arm pits, when Trout fell off the roof of his house. Trout then climbed into a tree to keep from being swept away in the flooding river. Miller reached higher ground, then shouldering his rifle, shot Trout from the tree. It was first reported that J.R. Trout was killed, but he did recover. A Jo Gunter was also suspected as the man who had shot and wounded Jasper Trout. Miller was arrested for the crime, but charges were later dropped due to a lack of evidence.[13]

Ed Hendricks, a local tough from the Chickasaw Nation, was a frequent and obnoxious visitor to the Corner Saloon. It had been reported to the authorities that the saloon employees had been delivering whiskey into Indian Territory. Hookey thought that Hendricks was the party who had made the report. In early July 1905, Ed Hendricks again appeared at the Corner Saloon.

On that occasion trouble immediately developed between the bartender and the patron from the Chickasaw Nation. Each pulled a pistol and fired. Hendricks' shot missed, but Hookey's didn't. Hendricks was hit in the side and started running from the saloon. Miller then threw his pistol aside, grabbed a rifle from under the bar, and followed the fleeing man. When Hookey stepped out of the door, Hendricks shot at him. Hookey then fired twice at his wounded adversary, who was hiding behind a tree. Within a few minutes Ed Hendricks was dead with three bullets in his body. Miller was later arrested by Pottawatomie County sheriff W.A. Grace.[14]

A preliminary hearing was held at Tecumseh in mid-July 1905 on the charge of Miller murdering Ed Hendricks.

Judge Durham ruled that Miller was to be bound over to await action of the grand jury and established that his bond would be one thousand dollars. Miller posted bond and was transferred from the Pottawatomie County jail to the Chickasaw Nation, where he also faced charges. Judge Talbott held a hearing at Ada in late July on two charges against Miller for introducing liquor into Indian Territory. He was bound over for trial and released after posting a five-hundred-dollar bond on each count, plus a five-hundred-dollar peace bond, "all returnable on October 2, 1905."[15]

Over a year later, in November 1906, George Miller was arrested at Custer City. The Hendricks murder case was still pending, and he had skipped bond. He was taken to Hobart where his bond was increased. His brother furnished the revised bond, and Hookey was released again.[16]

From Hobart, Miller again disappeared from the Oklahoma scene. According to information from his family, he returned to Texas about 1907. He and his sons then located on a place in Motley County, where the boys cleared the land and Hookey sold wood and did some wagon freighting. This continued for about three years, then Miller moved to Oklahoma City. Ed and George Jr. followed later. The sons married, settled in the Oklahoma City area, and started raising their families. One living granddaughter can remember Hookey as a doting grandfather. She recalls occasions when he and a lady friend visited her father Ed and family, when they lived at Norman.[17]

The whereabouts and activities of Hookey Miller for the next several years remain mostly unknown. Some of the notes he left behind indicate that he spent some of that time in Pontotoc County, looking for Will Hendricks (a brother of Hookey's victim, Ed) against whom Hookey still carried a grudge.[18]

The next confirmed account of Miller was 1923, in Kay County, Oklahoma. The Tonkawa oil field in the southern part of that county was one of the most recent strikes and fastest growing areas in the country. In the midst of the booming oil field the town of Three Sands sprang up. The new town extended south into Noble County. Kay County deputy sheriff John Middleton, who was known as "Two Gun John," was assigned to Three Sands. Two Gun John had derived his sobriquet from "his swaggering with two large guns hanging from his hips." He was very active as a officer, but controversial in carrying out his duties.

Three Sands was typical of the oil boom towns in Oklahoma. Soon it was filled with low-life characters of all descriptions. While Two Gun John enjoyed great popularity in the sheriff's office and among certain of the residents, he was however considered by many to be inclined to enforce the law selectively. Neither oil field workers nor Indians were considered to be among his favored lot. One newspaper article described Two Gun John as "having a braggadocio spirit, beating up and browbeating the inoffensive."[19]

As criminal activity continued to increase at Three Sands, Kay County deputy sheriff Hookey Miller was assigned to assist Deputy Middleton in maintaining law and order. Two Gun John had previously arrested a drunken oil field worker by the name of Jackson Burns and had taken a quantity of "choc" (homebrewed beer) from him. Since there was no jail at Three Sands, the deputy chained Burns, who was a Choctaw Indian and called "Chief" by his fellow workers, to a bedstead in a rooming house until he sobered up. This initial encounter was followed by several other incidents that led to great enmity between Jackson Burns and Deputy Middleton. Miller had not been involved in any of the conflicts between Chief Burns and Two Gun John Middleton; however, he was present when the showdown came.

According to witnesses, Deputies Middleton and Miller were walking along Three Sand's main street about noon on July 21, 1923. As they passed the Wayside Cafe, Two Gun John spotted Chief Burns inside. The Indian was sitting at a table near the front of the cafe waiting to be served. Middleton was heard saying to Miller, "There is the son-of-a-bitch, now," and Miller replied, "Let's smoke him out." Jackson Burns saw the two deputies reach for their weapons as they approached the screen door to enter. Realizing that they were after him, the Indian stood, pulled his .38-caliber pistol, and started firing at the officers. Miller went down immediately, with three slugs in his body. Middleton was hit once, then turned and fled. Burns stepped out the door, over Miller, and shot the running deputy twice more. Two Gun John then fell to the ground.[20]

It was reported that Hookey stated, "I would like to live long enough to take a shot at that 'yellow' Middleton," shortly before he died while en route to the Tonkawa hospital. Two Gun John died the following day. Miller's younger son was living in Oklahoma City at the time his father was killed. George Jr. went to Tonkawa and returned with his father's body. He then arranged for his father's funeral at the Capital Hill Funeral Parlor. George D. "Hookey" Miller was buried in the Rose Hill Cemetery, in northwest Oklahoma City. Middleton's body was shipped to Santa Cruz, California, for burial.[21]

Immediately after the shooting, Jackson Burns went to Newkirk, the county seat of Kay County, and surrendered to the jailer (the sheriff was out of town, trying to find the man who had killed his deputies). Burns claimed that he had fired in self-defense, as he thought that the two officers intended to kill him. "Oil men and business men of Three Sands...offered a bond of more than one hundred thousand dollars for his release, as he was popular and a favorite in the field and a good worker."[22]

Jackson Burns was tried at Newkirk for the murder of Two Gun John Middleton and found not guilty on September 28, 1923. The case against the Indian oil field worker for the murder of Miller was still pending at that time, but the prosecutor was seriously considering dropping the case. He reasoned that the evidence in Miller's case was the same as he had presented in Middleton's case, and it had not convinced the jury to convict Burns of murder.[23] Likely, the case was dropped, as further information has not been located.

It appears that Hookey Miller was never tried for any of the crimes with which he had been charged in Oklahoma Territory and, in turn, while an officer of the law in Oklahoma, was killed in the line of duty by a man who was not tried for his murder.

When the recently discovered oil field was drilled out, the rigs moved on, and the boom at Three Sands was over. Within a few years, as the very productive shallow wells began to weaken and dry up, the town did also. Today, only a cemetery and a few building foundations remain at the site of the once flourishing town of Three Sands.

CHAPTER 26

Still More Trouble
for the Hughes Brothers

As the twentieth century dawned, the Hughes ranch on the Washita continued to grow and prosper. Farming activities had increased until twenty-five thousand bushels of corn were harvested annually. Other crops of the farming and ranching operation were similarly productive. The Hughes brothers had not only obtained the contract for "the star route mail delivery," but they had also negotiated for the lease of thirty-six sections of "Indian Land" in the area. Jim and Ben Hughes were each thought to be worth in excess of one hundred thousand dollars, which if expressed in the monetary value of a century later would represent two million dollars apiece.

Their land purchases had added some seven sections of deeded property to the senior Hughes' original homestead. Their land and the leased Indian land were not in a solid tract, but had they been, the ranch would have exceeded an area seven miles long and six miles wide. Their ranch abutted the Caddo County line on the east. This large expanse of land permitted some of their operations to be conducted beyond the prying eyes of their neighbors. Their partial seclusion, however, had not prevented those living for miles around from becoming suspicious of and well stocked with rumors to the effect that the ranch was an outlaw haven and to some extent served mainly as a ploy for the benefit of "men on the dodge."

The Hughes brothers were never well accepted by the home-steaders in the area; however, there were a few nesters who glo-ried for their favor and who would ride day or night to alert them of a posse approaching their ranch. The warnings that these messengers delivered frequently provided the men the Hughes brothers referred to as their "dugout boys" and who were hiding out on the ranch an opportunity to escape from the oncoming lawmen.

Common talk that had circulated in the area about their past had put their neighbors on alert as to the nature of the Hughes brothers. The fast expansion of their ranch and the scope of their operations set them apart from the other farmers in the community and created suspicion. Many of the homesteaders throughout the Territory had suffered great hardships merely to eke out an existence on the new land, which had caused mass skepticism and perhaps envy toward the Hughes. As the county lawmen's searches for Bert Casey continued to lead them to the Hughes ranch, only to find each time that Casey had escaped again, the local citizens and officers began to let their feelings be known and their voices be heard.

"On August 8, 1902, a crowd of citizens led by sheriffs from Caddo, Kiowa and Washita counties, went to the ranch homes of Jim and Ben Hughes and notified them that they would be shot or hanged if they did not leave Oklahoma Territory." It was shortly after this confrontation that Marshal Fossett released Hudson and Lockett from the Federal jail at Guthrie and sent them to "get Bert Casey."

A few months later, "March 29, 1903, sheriffs from five coun-ties, Caddo, Kiowa, Washita, Garfield and Canadian, combined posses and searched the ranch for dead bodies, outlaws and the Hughes brothers. The posses went to the extreme of exca-vating a deep well, which they found had been filled and in which they believed dead bodies would be found."[1]

Being charged with the murder of Deputy Marshal Lute Hous-ton had furthered suspicion and resentment toward the Hughes brothers. Amid the frequent interferences and numerous

Depicted as a scene at the Hughes ranch. (Copyright, 1995, Oklahoma Publishing Company. From the September 4, 1932, issue of *The Daily Oklahoman.*)

arrests by the officers and the clamor of the citizenry, the Hughes brothers lost their lease of the "Indian Land" and their contract for "carrying the mail." These divestitures, along with the death in 1904 of their father, James Hughes Sr., who had been the ranch's most stable force, set in motion the breakup of the "Hughes Ranch On The Washita." As their ranch holdings crumbled away, the Hughes brothers continued to have troubles with the law. After they were freed in 1906 of the charges against them for the murder of Lute Houston, each of the aged brothers was charged with separate crimes later in life.

In the latter part of 1907, an unusual robbery of a store in Arapaho occurred, which ultimately led to Ben Hughes being tried for the crime. Tom Hartgraves of Clinton was the first man tried for the robbery, and the local newspaper reported in March 1908 the following account: "The history of the case reads like a romance. It is the theory of the prosecution that a well planned system of robberies was perpetrated on our fellow townsman and merchant J.D. Simpson. It is Mr. Simpson's belief that there was taken from his store from $1000. to $1500. worth of clothing, shoes, silks and valuable stuff, that was not too bulky to carry. Now, it is contended that this did not happen in one night, or in a week, but was carefully planned and so concealed that it was some time before it was discovered. The theory goes that the robbers had a key and entered the front door of the store. It was not the contention of the prosecution that the defendant entered the store, but was a beneficiary, and had some of the goods in his possession."

The article continued: "It developed during the trial that the lawyers for the prosecution had been offered a hundred dollar bill and the finest suit in town, just to let one man stay on the jury. This brought on a quarrel and almost a personal matter out side the court room, from the fellows who thought that the lawyers were disgracing the profession, by not making a little easy money, when they had the chance." The jury could not reach a decision, and the trial was rescheduled for a later date.[2]

The second trial of Tom Hartgraves was held in November 1908 at Arapaho. The prosecution produced a Charles White,

Street scene, Arapaho, Oklahoma, circa 1910. (Courtesy of Custer County State Bank, Arapaho, Oklahoma.)

who was there as a witness and to turn state's evidence. White had been convicted of arson at Anadarko. He was serving a sentence at Lansing, Kansas, for that crime, when returned by the state for the Hartgraves trial. White admitted being involved with the gang that stole the goods from the Simpson store, also the Dixie store in Weatherford. He revealed where the burglar keys could be found, under a house in Cordell, and where most of the stolen goods were hidden. The information proved to be right. Some of the stolen goods had been found in Hartgraves' home and saloon at Clinton.

White's testimony was well received by the jury. On November 25, 1908, the court found Tom Hartgraves "guilty of receiving stolen goods." "White acknowledged that he had been a member of the Hughes gang and knew of some of their operations. He claimed that they had framed him on the arson charge. White let it be known that he was ready to reveal information about some of the Hughes gang's activities, because of their betrayal of him."[3]

Ben Hughes was brought to trial at Arapaho, in July 1909, for involvement in the robbery of the Simpson store. A newspaper account of the trial referred to the Hughes ranch on the Washita as being regarded for several years as a "rendezvous for thieves and outlaws." Charles White was again called as the main witness for the state. The defense produced several witnesses who testified to the good character of Hughes and degraded that of White. They claimed that Ben was innocent and that White was the guilty party. Again, Charles White proved to be a very persuasive witness. On July 20, 1909, the jury found Ben Hughes guilty, and the district court sentenced him to four years in prison. A motion by the defense for a new trial was overruled, and the case was processed to the state appeals court.[4]

The conviction of Ben Hughes delighted many people of the area, whether their cause to resent the Hughes brothers was real or imagined. One newspaper, choosing to continue with the currently popular subject of ridiculing Ben Hughes, reported that "he had become a good lawyer, because of his many experiences in court." The article related about Bert Casey's association with the Hughes brothers, then went on to rehash some of the crimes that they had been charged with. It told about Lute Houston's murder, "and the resulting trials, at which the people were afraid to testify. Ben Hughes had never dressed-up until he had that trial. At that trial in which Ben Hughes came clear, he appeared in a new suit of store clothes, which he wore from then on, until they were worn out."

The article reported that the Hughes brothers were "politically powerful, that Ben had ran for Sheriff in Washita county and that the brothers had made fortunes, which they used to make themselves popular in Custer county." It pointed out that "any man who opposed them was ridiculed, threatened and his property stolen and usually got arrested himself, just to teach him, 'how mighty was their gang.'"[5]

A man whose name was reported in the newspapers only as V. Camp was brought to trial in November 1910 at Arapaho. He became the third man convicted of the Simpson store robbery. The newspaper reporter took another swipe at Ben Hughes who had attended the trial by describing his manner of dress as follows: "Ben invariably wears one shoe and one boot. A pair of blue work pants, that keep the wits scared out of his closest friends for fear they will fall for lack of suspenders. A good white Stetson is set carelessly on his head. His only ornament is a cob pipe. Jim Hughes is dressed more like other people."[6]

While Ben was awaiting a hearing of his larceny conviction by the state appeals court, another story of his past surfaced: "Some years ago Ben Hughes had a firm of merchants as friends, Stinson & Lamberson, of Cloud Chief. Later the firm moved to Mountain View and the opportunity to get goods for nothing presented itself, so he bought a coupon book. Then Ben hiked to Chickasha where he had friends in the printing business and he had a large supply of coupon books printed. Then, Ben drew the goods and nearly busted the firm."[7]

A motion to grant V. Camp a new trial was heard in late December 1910, but the request was denied. At the time of that hearing, Ben Hughes and V. Camp were circulating a petition for a pardon from Governor Charles Haskell. The newspaper reported, "Ben says that 'He don't pretend to have been any angel, in the past, but he hates like hell to go to the penitentiary.' He has a remarkable following in Custer county and will likely get consideration, as Governor Haskell don't seem inclined to leave anybody in the pen."[8]

At that time, it seems that Ben Hughes was the most controversial subject in western Oklahoma. A rumor was circulated in January 1911 that Governor Haskell had signed Ben's pardon as one of his last acts and had left it for incoming Governor Lee Cruce to issue. The resentment created by the rumored Hughes pardon was somewhat tempered with the story that Oklahoma officials had obtained a pardon for Charles White, for his testimony in the three cases.[9]

Ben Hughes had over the years beaten the many cases that had been brought against him. The previous charges had included larceny of horses in the Chickasaw Nation, two counts of robbing trains in Texas, and two separate cases of murdering a deputy U.S. marshal (one in each of the Twin Territories), without serving any prison time. He had been successful in defending himself against major criminal charges in three states, but he was not able to beat the case of his accused involvement in stealing some clothes from the Simpson Dry Goods Store at Arapaho.

Ben Hughes was received at the Oklahoma State Penitentiary on April 27, 1911, as prisoner Number 2609. He was to serve a four-year sentence for the crime of "grand larceny" in Custer County. At the time that he entered prison, he was listed as fifty years of age. Ben reported that his wife's name was Ida and that he owned and had farmed 160 acres of land at Cloud Chief, Oklahoma. It soon became apparent that Ben was not without friends who wielded certain influence. After serving only five months of the four-year sentence, he secured a parole and was released on September 20, 1911.[10]

Ben's older brother Jim stayed out of trouble with the law

for several years following the murder charge for which he was acquitted in 1906, but later he too was arrested, charged, tried, and convicted of another crime. On May 22, 1922, Jim Hughes was arrested at Cloud Chief, Oklahoma. He was charged with violation of the National Motor Vehicle Theft Act (transporting a stolen automobile across a state line), commonly referred to at that time as the "Dyer Act."

The older Hughes brother managed to delay the trial for about a year, but in October 1923 his case was called in the Western District of Oklahoma. Jim Hughes was convicted and sentenced on November 7, 1923, to serve four years in the Federal penitentiary. He appealed his conviction and was released on bond until the hearing. The appeals court upheld the conviction, and James S. Hughes entered the prison at Leavenworth, Kansas, August 18, 1925, as Number 23887. Jim reported to the officials that his residence had been Cloud Chief, Oklahoma, that he was a widower, that he had two sons, and that in case of sickness or death to contact an Ellis Ringo of Cloud Chief.

Jim Hughes was sixty-seven years old when he was received into the federal prison system. His age set him apart from most of the inmates. Upon his arrival at Leavenworth he was given a light duty assignment, but was soon charged with violation of prison rules. He was then reprimanded and assigned to the brick yard. Due to Jim's age and the condition of his health, he was relieved from that work and permitted to spend his time "idle in cell." This later led to another physician's report to the warden stating, "He is an old man, who is in rather a dilapidated physical condition. He has been 'idle in cell' for about a year and I do not believe he is getting the fresh air and exercise that his condition demands." At one time he was transferred to the "hog farm" so he could sleep outdoors. Over the many months of his confinement he was given numerous assignments, the longest of which was work in the library, with full yard privileges.

When a young man, Jim had stood six feet tall, and while in prison he weighed but 142 pounds. His prison medical records show that he had a "heart condition" and a "crippled left front toe."

The inmate's age, health, and attitude caused much concern for the prison's supervisors, physicians, and warden.

He was denied parole at his first eligibility hearing, in December 1926. Nine months later, he again failed to gain approval of the board. One year later, on September 15, 1928, after serving thirty-seven months of the four-year sentence, he was granted a parole. According to the provisions of his parole, Jim Hughes was to return to Cloud Chief where he was to work for Ellis Ringo (recorded as the parolee's "First Friend") for his board and twenty-five dollars per month.[11]

Sometime after Ben Hughes was released from the Oklahoma prison in 1911, he moved from the farm near Cloud Chief to a farm at the eastern edge of Roger Mills County, about eight miles north of Hammon. During the summer of 1932, officers from Oklahoma and Kansas raided his farm in Roger Mills County. The Kansas officers were searching for automobiles that had been stolen from that state, and the Oklahoma officials were searching for bank robbers.

The officers found neither the cars nor the robbers, but did uncover a stash of buried whiskey. The seventy-two-year-old Hughes still had an alert mind and a knack for displaying his craftiness. He explained that a "moonshiner" never buried his wares on his own property, but that of a neighbor; and if it had been his whiskey, that he would have hidden it somewhere other than on his own farm. Ben readily acknowledged his taste for liquor and offered the officers a "nip," if he could find any around his house. The officers dropped the matter and left his farm without filing any charges against him.[12]

A few weeks after the officers from Oklahoma and Kansas visited Ben's farm near Moorewood, Oklahoma, a three-part series appeared in the *Daily Oklahoman*. The articles recounted some of the troubles with the law that the Hughes brothers had incurred over the years. The series was written by Alvin Rucker, staff writer of the *Sunday Oklahoman*, and was titled "When Banditry Was In Flower." The three articles were published in the Sunday edition of the *Daily Oklahoman* of September 4, 11, 18, 1932.

Ben and Jim Hughes, circa 1930. (From the author's collection.)

Rucker reported that at that time Jim Hughes owned a valuable but heavily mortgaged hotel in Sentinel, Oklahoma, and had another car case pending.

CHAPTER 27

The Next Generation

Robert Hughes was called "Rob" by his father Jim Hughes, and was known as "Bob" in the community. He lived near his well-known father's ranch, in eastern Washita County, and used some of the ranch's equipment in his independent farming operation. On September 1, 1910, Jim Hughes and a hired hand harnessed the horses and hitched the teams to three wagons to haul some grain from near Rob's farm to Jim's place. It was planned that the son was to come over to his dad's place that morning and drive one of the teams, but the son did not arrive at the ranch. Jim then asked his father-in-law, Jim Lewis, to fill in for Rob and drive the third team. Lewis agreed, and the three men drove the wagons to the site and proceeded to load the grain.

When they discovered that one of the wagons leaked grain and was not suitable for the job, Jim Hughes and his father-in-law went to Rob's place, to exchange the faulty wagon for one at his son's home. A row developed between Rob and his father over the ownership of the wagons involved. The quarrel became more heated as it extended to a previously agreed, but not yet completed, grain transaction between Jim Hughes and his son.[1]

The senior Hughes proceeded with his plan to leave the defective wagon and hitch the team to another, in defiance of his son's protests. Rob then went into his house and returned with a shotgun. Holding the weapon "at ready," he threatened Jim Hughes' life if he continued his course of hitching the team to the other wagon. Lewis interposed on behalf of his son-in-law and shamed Rob about threatening to kill his own father. As Lewis was speaking, Rob looked in his direction and turned the weapon accordingly. The intervening Lewis' close approach to the young man was met by a shotgun blast which blew away the old man's jaw. Lewis died a few minutes later. Bob Hughes was arrested, charged with murder of Jim Lewis, and held in the Cordell jail.[2]

A week after Lewis was shot and killed, a preliminary trial was held at Cordell. Jim Hughes was the main witness called at the hearing. His testimony provided the details of the incident as previously described, and his son Rob was bound over for trial.[3]

About six weeks later, Bob Hughes was tried for the murder of his father's father-in-law, Jim Lewis. The trial was held at Cordell, and the jury acquitted Hughes on October 22, 1910. After a brief announcement of the acquittal, the newspaper article continued by reporting about some of the previous associates and incidents with which the Hughes brothers, Jim and Ben, had been involved.[4]

A decade later, in October 1920, a car owned by Bert Evans was stolen at Weatherford, in Custer County. Sheriff Monroe learned that the suspect, Ben Hughes Jr., and the stolen car were at Sentinel, in southern Washita County. On October 24, 1920, Washita County sheriff John Miller and Custer County sheriff Monroe located and arrested Ben Hughes Jr. for the crime.[5]

Ben Hughes Jr. was the son of the noted Ben Hughes and was sometimes referred to as "Raleigh" and "Little Ben," then later in his career merely as "Ben Hughes." Little Ben's trial was held at Arapaho, and he was convicted of "larceny of an automobile." He was sentenced to serve five years in prison. Ben Jr. was transported from the Custer County jail to the prison facility at Granite on November 26, 1920. He was received at Granite as "Ben

Hughes," age twenty-two, and became prisoner Number 2768. His inmate record card shows that he was paroled on October 29, 1921, but on March 15, 1923, his parole was revoked.[6]

Apparently he did not return to prison when his parole was revoked, because in July 1923, Ben Jr., then using an alias of "Ray Williams," was arrested and jailed at Enid. Within a few days he broke out of that lockup. He was captured a week later at Ponca City and was returned to the Enid jail. Two days after being returned to that place of security, Ben again escaped. Two other prisoners accompanied him in his second break.[7]

Sometime later, Little Ben was recaptured and returned to prison to serve the remainder of his five-year sentence. He gained approval for parole and was released on April 7, 1925.[8]

On July 28, 1926, the State Bank at Corn, Oklahoma, was robbed. A short time after the robbery, the Chevrolet touring car that had been used in the getaway was found burning, nine miles south of Corn, on the Washita River. Some papers taken from the bank at the time of the robbery were recovered from the burned automobile, which had been stolen at Carnegie the night before. Little Ben and his younger brother John, sons of the noted Ben Hughes were seen leaving the area of the burning car. The brothers were arrested, questioned by officers, and released. They were later arrested again and charged with the bank robbery.

The town of Corn is located in northeastern Washita County, and a hearing for the Hughes brothers was held at Cordell on August 10, 1926. P.B. Harms, president of the bank, who had been forced to lie upon the floor while the bandits took the money, positively identified Ben Jr. as one of the robbers. P.D. Gantzen, a customer who entered the bank while the holdup was taking place, testified that he believed the Hughes boys were the ones who committed the robbery. Little Ben and John took the stand in their own defense and produced witnesses to account for their whereabouts at the exact time of the incident. District judge E.L. Mitchell was not impressed by the brothers' alibi. He bound them over for trial and set bond for each at eight thousand dollars. Little Ben was reported to be about twenty-seven years old, and John was about eighteen.[9]

A few days later, six men signed the bond for John Hughes, and he was released to await trial. No documents relative to his trial have been located. It may be presumed that he was acquitted, or if convicted his sentence was suspended, as there is no record of John Hughes having been sent to an Oklahoma prison.[10]

Federal officers arrived at Cordell to take Little Ben into custody, but since they did not have a warrant, Sheriff John Miller refused to give him up. The officers declared that he was wanted on five charges, among them a jail break at Enid and one at Guthrie, also he had a "white slavery" charge pending.[11]

Ben Hughes Jr. was convicted of the Corn State Bank robbery and sentenced to five years in prison. His attorneys filed an appeal for a new trial. Judge Mitchell ruled against the new trial, but did reduce the bond requirement to five thousand dollars. Little Ben's mother, Ida Hughes, and a friend of the family, Jeff Moore, signed the bond. Ben Jr. was then released to await a review of his case by the Court of Criminal Appeals.[12]

Little Ben's parole for the larceny of an automobile conviction was revoked by Governor Martin E. Trapp on December 13, 1926.[13] He was returned to Granite to serve the remainder of his previous sentence. On November 20, 1928, Ben stole a state-owned car that was delivering the mail to the prison and "got away."[14]

Not only did Ben Hughes made good his escape from the state prison, by stealing a state vehicle, but he could not be located by officers. About a week after he had fled, the Court of Criminal Appeals dismissed his appeal that had been pending on his bank robbery conviction. The appeals court also issued an order for the bondsmen to produce the felon, or forfeit the five-thousand-dollar "supersedeas" bond. Mrs. Ida Hughes and Jeff Moore, cosigners of the bond, were notified to produce the escapee no later than Monday morning, December 2, 1928, or the bond would be called. As the zero hour approached, the "wanted man" appeared before district judge E.L. Mitchell. Ben Hughes Jr. was returned that evening to Granite, to continue serving the remainder of his time for stealing the car, plus the five-year sentence for robbing the Corn State Bank.[15]

Ben Jr. was transferred from Granite to McAlester on September 9, 1931. His inmate card shows that he was granted a leave of absence from October 12, 1931, to December 23, 1931. Another leave of absence is recorded to have started December 23, 1931, and was to expire June 1, 1932. Another entry shows that the leave was revoked on May 18, 1932 (two weeks before it was due to expire). Obviously, Ben did not return to prison when his parole was revoked. In all likelihood he was the bank robber being sought by the Oklahoma officers when they, along with Kansas officials who were looking for stolen cars, raided his father's farm in the summer of 1932.

In the early morning hours of September 14, 1932, the home of Horace B. Tharp in Amarillo, Texas, exploded. The Tharps were not at home at the time, but the bodies of two unidentified men were found in the wreckage. The police found a car loaded with furnishings from the home, abandoned about two blocks from the house. A neighbor reported that he had seen two men with a gasoline can going toward the house, then heard the explosion, and immediately saw a man drive a car away.

The bodies of the two men that had been found at the site of the explosion were put on display, and the public was invited to come and observe, in the hopes that someone would be able the identify their remains. A Mrs. Passmore of Elk City, Oklahoma, was visiting her sister-in-law, Mrs. W.C. Ellis, in Amarillo when the mysterious blast occurred. In response to the solicitation of the police, hundreds of local citizens went to view the bodies. Mrs. Passmore and Mrs. Ellis decided to visit the currently popular downtown attraction.

The two women were startled to recognize one of the bodies as that of J.C. Passmore. J.C. was the husband of the lady from Elk City, and the brother of Mrs. Ellis. J.C. Passmore was a twenty-six-year-old Oklahoman, having been raised in the Sweetwater community near the Beckham and Roger Mills county line.

Mrs. Passmore reported that when her husband had left their home a few days earlier, he had said that he was going to Leedey, Oklahoma, to look for a job and a place to live. The women were positive in their identification of their loved one. They were uncertain about the other man; however, they suggested that he might be Ben Hughes. Upon confirmation of J.C. Passmore's identity, his remains were released to his wife, and he was buried at Sayre, Oklahoma.[16]

When the Hughes family received word that Ben Jr. might have been one of the victims in the explosion, John Hughes went to Amarillo. John confirmed the identity of his older brother and was permitted to return Little Ben's remains to his home state. Information concerning the identification of the two Oklahomans who had been killed in the Amarillo house explosion was received by the Oklahoma newspapers at the same time as the third installment of Alvin Rucker's series about the senior Ben Hughes and his brother Jim was being published on September 18, 1932. Rucker did not mention the recent demise of Ben Jr. nor any of the troubles with the law that the sons of the senior Hughes brothers had encountered.

An undated annotation on Ben Hughes' inmate card reads: "Fugitive, Killed in explosion in Amarillo, Texas."[17] Ben Hughes Jr. was buried near the grave of his mother Ida, who had died two years previously. His father lived another thirteen years. Lacking but four months reaching eighty-five years of age, the senior Ben Hughes succumbed to death on June 5, 1945.[18]

Ben was buried beside his wife Ida and, in 1978, their son John was buried but a few feet away. The graves of Ben, Ida, Ben Jr., and John are in the Moorewood Cemetery, near the northwestern corner of Custer County.

Jim Hughes lived more than twenty years after he was released from prison for the auto theft conviction. At the age of ninety, Jim died in 1949. He was buried in the Oakdale Cemetery, near Mountain View, Oklahoma. The changes that had

Ben Hughes, Jr. Jan. 31, 1902 Sept. 14, 1932. Cemetery at Moorewood, Oklahoma.
(From the author's collection.)

Ida E. Hughes, 1873-1930. Ben F. Hughes, 1860-1945. Cemetery at Moorewood,
Oklahoma. (From the author's collection.)

J.S. (Jim) Hughes, 1858-1949. Oakdale Cemetery, Mountain View, Oklahoma.
(From the author's collection.)

come to pass between the years when James Hughes, Sr., was an associate of Kit Carson, exploring the "Far West" with John C. Frémont, and those which had been witnessed by his son James Jr. ("Jim"), who lived through the period of World War II, cover a vast span of our Western history.

Chronology of Homicides

1863	Willis Brooks Sr. was killed by seven vigilantes in Alabama. His son was killed a few days later.
April 1884	Gaines Brooks and two deputies were killed in a gun battle in Alabama.
May 21, 1894	Jim and Vic Casey killed Deputy Sam Farris in Canadian County.
Feb. 27, 1895	Ben Hughes killed Deputy Jim Nakedhead in the Creek Nation.
June 30, 1895	Police Chief Milton Jones and escaping inmate Jim Casey were killed during a jail break at Oklahoma City.
Sept. 1895	Gus Holland was killed in Dewey County.
Oct. 8, 1895	Ed Jennings was killed when he and his brother John were in a gunfight with Temple Houston and Jack Love in a saloon at Woodward.
Dec. 31, 1895	Lawmen killed Joe Beckham in Comanche country.

Feb. 14, 1896 George "Red Buck" Weightman and George Miller killed W.W. Glover, near Arapaho, Custer County.

Mar. 5, 1896 A sheriff's posse killed George "Red Buck" Weightman and shot off George Miller's right hand in Custer County.

Apr. 24, 1896 Tom Brooks was killed by a former Texas Ranger in the Creek Nation.

Nov. 7, 1897 A posse killed Dan "Dynamite Dick" Clifton in the Creek Nation.

Apr. 6, 1898 A posse killed "Little Dick" West near Guthrie.

Nov. 9, 1900 Deputy Sam Baker killed Bob Gentry at Checotah.

Mar. 10, 1901 Bert Casey and Tom Powers killed Rufus Choat near Youngs Crossing, Chickasaw Nation.

Aug. 4, 1901 The Bert Casey gang killed Jay Beemblossom in Comanche County.

Jan. 15, 1902 Sheriff Frank Smith and Deputy George Beck were killed by the Casey Gang in Caddo County.

Feb. 21, 1902 A sheriff's posse killed Walter Swofford (member of the Casey Gang) in the Seminole Nation.

Mar. 1902 A Mr. Arnold was killed in the Chickasaw Nation by parties unknown; Bert Casey was the main suspect.

June 30, 1902 Sheriff Jackson Bullard and Deputy John Cogburn were killed on Dead Indian Creek in Roger Mills County.

Aug. 23, 1902 Deputy Marshal Frank Jones shot Sam Baker,

but killed George Howard by accident, at Checotah.

Sept. 22, 1902 Willis Brooks, Cliff Brooks, and "Old Man Riddle" were killed in a feud at Spokogee, Creek Nation.

Oct. 10, 1902 Jim McFarland was killed by an unknown ambusher in the Creek Nation.

Oct. 20, 1902 Deputy Lute Houston was lynched by Bert Casey and his cohorts near Swan Lake in Caddo County.

Nov. 3, 1902 Special Deputies Fred Hudson and Ed Lockett killed Bert Casey and Jim Sims at Cleo Springs.

Feb. 3, 1903 Wes Hudson killed Deputy Jim Keys at Jasper, Arkansas.

1904 Wes Hudson killed Henry Barchman near Forsythe, Missouri.

1905 Wes Hudson killed a Negro (name of the victim is unknown) near Mer Rouge, Louisiana.

July 5, 1905 George "Hookey" Miller killed Ed Hendricks at Corner, O.T.

May 23, 1906 Fred Hudson and Jim Bourland killed each other in an Anadarko saloon.

Feb. 18, 1908 J.C. and Robert Woodson killed Dr. Zeno Beemblossom at the doctor's farm near Oklahoma City.

May 19, 1908 Susie Pride was killed by Alf Hunter in Oklahoma City.

June 5, 1908 Sheriff George Garrison was killed by Alf Hunter in Blaine County.

Mar. 27, 1909 Deputies Herman Odom and Ed Baum were

killed in the "Crazy Snake Rebellion" near Pierce, Creek Nation.

Mar. 29, 1909   Deputy Sam Baker killed Charlie Coker and another (unidentified) Indian near Pierce, Creek Nation.

Apr. 8, 1910   Alf Hunter was hanged at Watonga.

Sept. 1, 1910   Bob Hughes killed his step-grandfather James Lewis near Cloud Chief, Washita County.

Oct. 7, 1911   C.P. and Will Torrans killed Sam Baker in Checotah.

Jan. 11, 1920   Henry Brooks was killed by officers in Alabama.

Oct. 9, 1921   Attorney Moman Pruiett killed Joe Patterson in Oklahoma City.

July 21, 1923   Jackson Burns killed Deputies George "Hookey" Miller and "Two Gun John" Middleton at Three Sands in Kay County.

Sept. 12, 1932   Ben Hughes Jr. and J.C. Passmore were killed in an explosion of a home at Amarillo, Texas.

Notes

Chapter 1: A Train Robbery in Texas

1. The *Fort Worth Gazette,* October 19, 1894, provided the general information about the robbery and spoke of it as "yesterday," but did not specify the date that it did occur. "On or about the 16th day of October 1894" is the date cited on an affidavit relative to the robbery, based on information provided by Mr. Lochaby, the section foreman.

These two sources raise a doubt as to the actual date of the robbery. The October 19, 1894, date is used here to be compatible with the date of the robbery that was cited in the newspaper accounts of actions that followed.

2. *Fort Worth Gazette,* October 21, 1894.

3. Ibid., October 19, 1894.

Chapter 2: Death of a Deputy in the Creek Nation

1. *Muskogee Phoenix,* March 2, 1895. Some accounts of Sam Farmer's role in this affair refer to him as having been a Texas and Pacific Railroad detective.

2. Each of the five Indian Nations had its own police force known as the "Lighthorsemen."

3. *Fort Worth Gazette,* March 3, 1895. The man Deputy Farmer referred to as both "Anderson" and "Silvers" was charged under the name "Judd South."

4. *Daily Oklahoman,* September 4, 1932.

5. *Muskogee Phoenix,* March 2, 1895. Had Hughes been Indian, as was Nakedhead, the murder case might have been handled under the tribal laws of the Creek Nation, the site of the crime. If either the "accused" or the "victim" of a crime in Indian Territory was "not Indian," the case came under the jurisdiction of the Western District of Arkansas, Federal Court, at Fort Smith, Arkansas, then commonly referred to as "Judge Parker's Court."

6. *Fort Worth Gazette.* The date on the paper is printed February 29, 1895, which was not a leap year; therefore, February had only twenty-eight days. The edition was likely the issue that was published for March 1, 1895.

Chapter 3: The Elusive Ben Hughes

1. Copies of telegrams sent to Marshal Crump at Fort Smith.

2. *Fort Worth Gazette,* March 3, 1895.

3. *Twelve Years in the Saddle for Law and Order on the Frontiers of Texas,* by W.J.L. Sullivan, Texas Ranger, Co. B, Frontier Batallion, private printing, Austin, 1909. Reissued by Buffalo-Head Press, New York, 1966, p. 17.

4. Copy of the murder indictment; *Daily Oklahoman,* September 4, 1932, the first of a three-part series titled "When Banditry Was in Flower," written by Alvin Rucker, staff writer for the *Oklahoman.*

5. Copies of the larceny indictment, bond, and warrants for Ben Hughes' arrest.

6. *El Reno Democrat,* May 21, 1896. A more detailed account of this gunfight and the life of Temple Houston may be found in the book *Temple Houston, Lawyer With a Gun,* by Glenn Shirley, University of Oklahoma Press, Norman, 1980.

7. *Daily Oklahoman,* September 4, 1932. Copy of an undated Fort Smith court clerk paper which listed three options for the jury of the murder trial. The "not guilty" option is signed by T.H. Hood, Foreman. The other two choices are lined through.

8. Ibid.

Chapter 4: Sam Baker, an Ally of the Law and the Lawless

1. *Footprints in the Indian Nations,* by Helen Starr and O.E. Hill, private printing, Muskogee, 1974, pp. 57-60.

2. *West of Hell's Fringe,* by Glenn Shirley, University of Oklahoma Press, Norman, 1978, pp. 406, 407, 413-15.

3. One of the main streets in Checotah is Gentry Avenue, named in honor of Bob's brother, William E. Gentry.

4. *Eufaula Indian Journal,* November 16, 1900.

5. *The Experiences of a Deputy U.S. Marshal of the Indian Territory,* by W.F. Jones, private printing, Tulsa, 1937. Reissued by Starr-Hill Associates, Muskogee, 1976, p. 17.

6. *Checotah Inquirer,* August 29, 1902.

7. *Eufaula Indian Journal,* September 26, 1902.

8. *Oklahoma State Capital,* September 26, 1902.

9. This condensed account of the "Crazy Snake Rebellion" and Sam Baker's role is based on: *Oklahoma City Times,* March 29,30, 1909; *Checotah Inquirer,* April 19, 1901, and February 28, 1902; *The Experiences of a Deputy U.S. Marshal of the Indian Territory,* by W.F. Jones; and *Footprints in the Indian Nations,* by Helen Starr and O.E. Hill.

10. *Mark of Heritage,* by Muriel H. Wright, George H. Shirk, and Kenny A. Franks, University of Oklahoma Press, Norman, 1976, p. 187.

11. *Checotah Times,* October 13, 1911.

12. Ibid., October 27, 1911.

13. Ibid., November 3, 1911.

14. Author's visit to the McIntosh County courthouse, at Eufaula, December 6, 1994.

Chapter 5: Vengeance to the Death

1. This account of the family, the Alabama feud, and the early years in the Creek Nation is based on the book *Footprints in the Indian Nations,* by Helen Starr and O.E. Hill, private printing, Muskogee, 1974, pp. 57-62. Also some information was provided by Edward Herring of Mt. Hope, Alabama.

2. *The Experiences of a Deputy U.S. Marshal of the Indian Territory,* by W.F. Jones, private printing, Tulsa, 1937. Reissued by Starr-Hill Associates, Muskogee, 1976, p. 16.

3. *Eufaula Indian Journal,* December 7, 1900.

4. Ibid., September 19, 1902.

5. "Showdown at Spokogee, I.T." by Samuel Cerro, in the May 1970 issue of *Golden West* magazine.

6. *Eufaula Indian Journal,* September 19, 1902.

7. Ibid., September 26, 1902.

8. Ibid., October 17, 1902.

9. *Oklahoma State Capital,* October 12, 1902.

10. "Showdown at Spokogee, I.T." by Samuel Cerro.

11. *Footprints in the Indian Nations,* by Helen Starr and O.E. Hill, private printing, Muskogee, 1974, p. 66.

12. *Anadarko Tribune,* May 19,26, 1905.

13. Letter to the author from Oklahoma Department of Corrections, dated May 3, 1995, with attachments.

14. *Haleyville* (AL) *Journal,* January 15, 1920; *Franklin* (AL) *Times,* January 16, 1920; *Footprints in the Indian Nations,* by Helen Starr and O.E. Hill, p. 67. Newspaper articles and information provided by Edward Herring, Mt. Hope, Alabama.

Chapter 6: The Casey Clan

1. Canadian County census records, dated June 17, 1890.

2. *Norman Transcript,* March 13, 1902. This article included a review of some of the crimes attributed to the Casey clan. It did have the relationship of Bert to other family members correct, as were the other events that could be checked.

3. *Daily Oklahoman,* June 6, 1894.

4. Ibid. A detailed account of this encounter and the death of Deputy Farris is included in the book, *West of Hell's Fringe,* by Glenn Shirley, University of Oklahoma Press, Norman, 1978, pp. 212, 213.

5. Ibid., June 6, 1894.

6. *Oklahoma State Capital,* August 25, 1894. Flora Quick (wife of Ora Mundis), who frequently wore men's clothes and stole horses, went by the name of Tom King. She broke out of the Oklahoma City jail on June 13, 1893. An account of this escape and other escapades of her checkered life are included in the book *West of Hell's Fringe,* by Glenn Shirley, pp. 54, 243-49, 307.

7. The *Oklahoma Times Journal,* November 13, 1894, reported that Vic

died in the poor house. Another newspaper merely commented that "his death will save Canadian County considerable money."

8. *Oklahoma State Capital,* July 1, 1895. The book *Black Jack Christian: Outlaw,* by Jeff Burton, Press of the Territorian, Santa Fe, 1967, provides a biography of Bill and Bob Christian.

9. *Daily Oklahoman,* September 11, 1932.

10. Stated census record, dated June 14, 1900.

11. Custer County court record, dated February 9, 1901.

Chapter 7: The Hughes Ranch and Bert Casey

1. Dates of birth for James Sr., Mary, and James Jr. ("Jim") are based upon the census records of 1900 for Washita County. Ben's death certificate and tombstone record that he was born in 1860. The 1920 census record for Washita County shows that he was sixty-three years old.

2. Deputy Farmer tracked the suspects of the 1894 train robbery to the Cloud Chief area, shortly after James Hughes Sr. had moved there.

3. More information about Weightman, Miller, and Jennings is found in the book *West of Hell's Fringe,* by Glenn Shirley, University of Oklahoma Press, Norman, 1978. An account of Ben Cravens' criminal career is provided in *Buckskin and Spurs, a Gallery of Frontier Rogues and Heroes* by Glenn Shirley, Hastings House Publishers, New York, 1958.

4. Most of the general information in this chapter is based on articles which appeared in the *Daily Oklahoman,* Sundays September 4 and 11, 1932. These articles were a part of a series titled "When Banditry Was in Flower," written by Alvin Rucker.

Chapter 8: The Murder of Rufus Choat

1. The Canadian River is sometimes referred to as the South Canadian to identify it from the North Canadian River.

2. Some of the information about "The Box" saloon is based on the book *Moman Pruiett, Criminal Lawyer,* author uncertain, published by Harlow Publishing Corporation of Oklahoma City in 1944, p. 156.

3. *Chickasaw Enterprise,* December 5, 1902.

4. *Daily Ardmoreite,* March 17, 1901. This article incorrectly gave the

victim's name as "Luther Shoot." Some of the articles that followed identified the murdered man as "Luther Choate," while other items show him as "William Choate." Later articles gave his name as "Rufus Choat," which the author assumes to be correct.

5. *Moman Pruiett, Criminal Lawyer,* author uncertain, pp. 156-57.

6. *Chickasaw Enterprise,* December 5, 1902.

7. *Daily Ardmoreite,* March 17, 1901.

Chapter 9: The Casey Gang

1. *Anadarko Daily News,* March 14, 1902. A request was submitted to the appropriate records office in July 1993 to confirm if Bert Casey had killed his captain while in the military. The author could not verify the name of the victim or the date of the incident, nor could he be positive about what name Bert Casey may have been using at the time. Limited to the non-specific information that could be furnished, the researcher at the archives was not able to locate any record of the event that had been reported in the cited local newspaper.

2. *Caddo County Times,* February 27, 1902.

3. *St. Louis Republican* (dateline Guthrie, OK), September 15, 1912.

4. *Daily Oklahoman,* July 11, 1920.

5. *Chickasha Daily Express,* September 27, 1901.

6. *Daily Oklahoman,* September 11, 1932, in an article titled "When Banditry Was in Flower," written by Alvin Rucker.

7. *Norman Transcript,* November 13, 1902. The article was based on the testimony of Dr. Zeno Beemblossom, the first witness called at the trial of George Moran.

Chapter 10: Chris Madsen Gets His Man

1. This chapter is a shortened version of the account furnished by Homer Croy in his book titled *Trigger Marshal, The Story of Chris Madsen,* Duell, Sloan and Pearce, New York, 1958, pp. 129-41. Croy's thirteen-page chapter, called "The Beemblossom Murder," is a rather amusing account of this adventure in Madsen's long career as a deputy U.S. marshal.

2. *Lawton Weekly Republican,* July 30, 1903.

Chapter 11: Dr. Beemblossom Becomes a Sleuth

1. *Daily Oklahoman,* February 19, 1908.

2. *Portrait & Biographical Record of Oklahoma,* no author listed, Chapman Publishing Company, Chicago, 1901, p. 848.

3. Oklahoma County Land Records.

4. *Portrait & Biographical Record of Oklahoma,* no author listed, p. 848.

5. *Daily Oklahoman,* February 19, 1908.

6. Ibid., July 11, 1920. Article by Fred Sutton.

7. *St. Louis Republican* (dateline Guthrie, OK), September 15, 1912. A like account of Beemblossom's trailing the outlaws was published in the *Daily Oklahoman* on July 11, 1920, in an article by Fred Sutton. With but slight changes the Sutton article was published in the November 1968 issue of *True Frontier,* titled "The Violent End of the Casey Gang" and written by Leola Lehman. The same story was repeated in the December 1970 issue of *Great West,* as "Bert Casey, Outlaw," with M.P. Lehman listed as author.

8. *Chickasaw Weekly Express,* May 1, 1903.

9. *Daily Oklahoman,* February 19, 1908.

10. *Oklahoma City Times,* September 19, 1909.

11. Ibid., December 1, 1910.

12. Ibid., November 27, 1910.

13. Ibid., November 28, 1910.

14. Ibid., December 1, 1910.

Chapter 12: Two Homicides and a Hanging

1. Information about the Garrison family and George's life prior to his moving into Indian Territory was provided to the author by Frankie Garrison Shipman of Oklahoma City, who is a great-niece of George W. Garrison.

2. *Oklahoma City Times,* June 6, 1908.

3. Ibid., June 8, 1908.

4. *Daily Oklahoman,* June 6, 1908.

5. *Oklahoma City Times,* June 9, 1908.

6. Ibid., June 8, 1908.

7. *Lexington* (OK) *Leader,* October 1, 1909.

8. Ibid. (dateline Oklahoma City), October 8, 1909.

9. *Watonga Herald,* October 21, 1909.

10. Ibid., April 14, 1910.

11. *Watonga Republican,* July 18, 1991.

Chapter 13: Caddo County Lawmen Killed

1. *Norman Transcript,* February 27, 1902.

2. *Anadarko Record,* February 28, 1902.

3. *Anadarko Tribune,* January 31, 1902.

4. *Hobart Republican,* January 24, 1902. In describing the location of where the lawmen were killed, some of the newspaper articles referred to the house as an "Indian hut," eight to ten miles west of Anadarko.

5. *Weekly Oklahoma State Capital,* November 8, 1902.

6. *Anadarko Record,* February 28, 1902.

7. *Caddo County Times,* February 13, 1902.

8. *Hobart Republican,* January 24, 1902.

9. *Chickasaw Enterprise,* January 16, 1902.

10. Ben Cravens was a well-known outlaw of that era. He had been convicted and incarcerated and had broken out of prison in Kansas. Casey and Cravens were the two most sought after outlaws in Oklahoma Territory, at that time.

11. *Anadarko Record,* February 28, 1902.

12. Gus Bobbitt became the victim of an ambush on February 28, 1908. The conflict that led to a feud and later the murder of Bobbitt is covered in the books *Shotgun for Hire,* by Glenn Shirley, University of Oklahoma Press, Norman, 1970, and *Four Men Hanging,* by Welborn Hope, Century Press, Oklahoma City, 1974.

13. *Daily Ardmoreite,* February 16, 1902.

14. *Anadarko Record,* February 28, 1902.

15. *Daily Ardmoreite,* February 16, 1902.

16. *Caddo County Times,* February 13, 1902.

17. *Shawnee Herald,* February 7, 1902.

18. *Chickasaw Enterprise,* February 20, 1902.

19. Ibid. The "rough country, to the north" was accepted to mean the brakes along the Canadian River, in the vicinity of the Corner Saloon and Youngs Crossing. The area was known to be infested by many men who were dodging the law.

20. *Norman Transcript,* February 27, 1902.

21. *Chickasaw Weekly Express,* October 23, 1903.

22. *Daily Ardmoreite,* January 24, 1902.

Chapter 14: O.T. Posse Overtakes Outlaws in the Seminole Nation

1. *Weekly Times Journal,* March 7, 1902.

2. *Norman Transcript,* February 27, 1902.

3. Several newspaper accounts of this gunfight mention that it occurred near "Wewoka Mound." There is no landmark in that area that is currently known by that name. Most of the newspaper articles speak of this shootout as happening eight or ten miles south of Wewoka. The *Anadako Record* of February 28, 1902, identified the location as being the Johnson farm. The *Weekly Times Journal* of March 7, 1902, stated that it was the home of a Negro man who had married a white woman.

4. *Shawnee Herald,* February 28, 1902.

5. Some of the newspaper articles describing this gunfight incorrectly identify Jones as the wounded deputy. George Stone was crippled for the remainder of his life, as a result of the gunshot which fractured his hips.

6. *Shawnee Herald,* February 28, 1902.

7. *Norman Transcript,* February 17, 1902.

8. *Shawnee Herald,* February 28, 1902.

9. *Weekly Times Journal,* March 17, 1902.

10. *Anadarko Record,* February 28, 1902.

11. *Norman Transcript,* February 27, 1902.

12. *Anadarko Record,* February 28, 1902.

13. *Shawnee Herald,* February 28, 1902.

14. *Anadarko Record,* February 28, 1902.

15. *Weekly Times Journal,* March 7, 1902.

16. *Hobart Weekly Chief,* May 13, 1903.

Chapter 15: Murder on Dead Indian Creek

1. During the fifteen years that Roger Mills County was part of Oklahoma Territory, Day County, the county seat of which was Grand, joined it on the north. When Oklahoma became a state, Day County was dissolved. That portion of Day County south of the Canadian River became part of Roger Mills County and the northern portion of it was absorbed into Ellis County. At the same time, the southern portion of the old Roger Mills County became part of the newly created Beckham County.

2. *Cheyenne Sunbeam,* July 4, 1902.

3. *Cordell Beacon,* July 9, 1902.

4. *Cheyenne Sunbeam,* July 4, 1902.

5. *Cordell Beacon,* July 9, 1902.

6. *Daily Oklahoman,* May 26, 1906.

7. *Mangum Star,* July 3, 1902. Their having been seen near Elk City indicated that they were riding in the direction of, and might be en route to, the Hughes ranch.

8. *Chickasaw Enterprise,* July 3, 1902.

9. *A Brief History of Roger Mills County,* by Nat M. Taylor, private printing, no city, not dated, circa 1950, p. 40.

10. The life story of Temple Houston is well covered in Glenn Shirley's biography of the colorful attorney titled *Temple Houston, Lawyer With a Gun,* University of Oklahoma Press, Norman, 1980.

11. *Norman Transcript,* August 14, 1902.

12. *Daily Oklahoman,* May 26, 1906.

13. *A Brief History of Roger Mills County,* by Nat M. Taylor, p. 40.

14. Roger Mills Country sheriff's logbook, reviewed by the author in February 1994.

Chapter 16: "Get Bert Casey"

1. *Cordell Weekly Beacon,* August 30, 1901. The deputy's name is also found spelled "Bottoms."

2. *Norman Transcript,* August 14, 1902.

3. *Cordell Weekly Beacon,* November 9, 1901.

4. Ibid., January 3, 1902; *Oklahoma State Capital,* November 8, 1902; *Daily Oklahoman,* September 4, 1932.

5. *Watonga Republican,* January 9, 1902.

6. *Anadarko Daily News,* March 14, 1902.

7. *Norman Transcript,* August 14, 1902.

8. *Mountain View Progress,* August 8, 1902.

9. *Oklahoma State Capital,* November 8, 1902.

10. *Anadarko Daily Democrat,* October 4, 1902; *Oklahoma State Capital,* October 8, 1902. Some of the newspaper articles about this encounter with the outlaws referred to the site as "Devil's Canyon," and other accounts identified the location as "Cedar Canyon."

11. *Oklahoma State Capital,* October 8, 1902.

Chapter 17: The Moment of Truth at Cleo Springs

1. Hudson, Lockett, Casey, and Sims were camped near the actual Cleo Springs. The name of the town was changed from Cleo to Cleo Springs in 1917.

2. *Weekly Oklahoma State Capital,* November 8, 1902, provides Fossett's account of the overall quest. Practically all the news articles about the adventure and gunfight were derived from the quoted article that was related by Fossett. None of the follow-up newspaper articles mentioned any interviews with or comments made by Hudson or Lockett.

3. Ibid. The reason for the large variance cited as the reward for Casey is because in a sheriffs association meeting at El Reno each of the thirty-five members present pledged to raise two hundred dollars for the reward. It was not known at the time Casey was killed how many of those pledges had been met.

4. Ibid.

5. *Purcell Register,* November 7, 1902.

6. The tombstone at the grave of Bert Casey incorrectly shows that the date of his death was November 8, 1902. He was killed on November 3 and buried on November 8, 1902.

Chapter 18: Deputy Lute Houston, a Victim of the Noose

1. *Trigger Marshal, The Story of Chris Madsen,* by Homer Croy, Duell, Sloan and Pearce, New York, 1958, p. 110.

2. *Mountain View Progress,* October 30, 1902.

3. *Chickasha Daily Express,* November 13, 1902.

4. *Daily Oklahoman,* April 25, 1903.

5. Swan Lake was a small body of water on Willow Creek, near where it flowed into Cobb Creek. When Cobb Creek was dammed, Swan Lake then became a part of Fort Cobb Lake. There is a small settlement near the original lake site that is still known as Swan Lake.

6. *Mountain View Progress,* April 2, 1903.

7. *Chickasha Weekly Express,* April 24, 1903. The article reported the proceedings of the preliminary hearing and the testimonies of the five witnesses.

8. Ibid. The grave of Luther "Lute" Houston is unmarked or illegible and cannot be located at this time. The currently available records of the cemetery do not extend to that early date.

Chapter 19: Territorial Courts and Trials

1. *Shawnee Herald,* July 29, 1902.

2. *Hobart Weekly Chief,* September 3, 1903.

3. *Moman Pruiett, Criminal Lawyer,* author uncertain, Harlow Publishing Corporation, Oklahoma City, 1944, pp. 176-77.

4. Oklahoma Historical Society, Oklahoma City, "The Fred Barde Collection," Scrapbook, Vol. 8., dated February 25, 1902, to September 20, 1902.

5. (Vinita) *Daily Chieftain,* November 6, 1902.

6. *Oklahoma State Capital,* November 8, 1902.

7. *Anadarko Daily Democrat,* November 18, 1902. After Quanah surrendered with his band of Comanches in 1875, he adopted most of the "white man's ways," except that he continued to claim his eight wives.

8. *Oklahoma State Capital,* November 8, 1902.

9. (Lawton) *Daily Republican,* November 1, 1902.

10. Ibid., November 3, 1902.

11. Ibid., November 10, 1902.

12. *Chickasha Weekly Express,* April 17, 1903.

13. Ibid., June 10, 1904.

14. Ibid., December 12, 1905.

15. Ibid., March 5, 1906.

Chapter 20: The Defense of Tom Powell

1. *Chickasaw Enterprise,* December 5, 1901.

2. *Moman Pruiett, Criminal Lawyer,* author uncertain, Harlow Publishing Corporation, Oklahoma City, 1944, pp. 156-65.

3. *Chickasaw Enterprise,* November 24, 1904.

4. *Moman Pruiett, Criminal Lawyer,* author uncertain, p. 65.

Chapter 21: Moman Pruiett, Attorney for the Defense

1. *Moman Pruiett, Criminal Lawyer,* author uncertain, Harlow Publishing Corporation, Oklahoma City, 1944, pp. 1-8.

2. Ibid., pp. 13-17.

3. Ibid., pp. 29-31.

4. Ibid., pp. 49-56.

5. Ibid., pp. 58-61.

6. *Daily Ardmoreite,* May 22, 1899.

7. This story was in the manuscript, but the main portion was deleted by Pruiett before the book was published.

8. *Daily Ardmoreite,* October 11, 1903.

9. *Pauls Valley Enterprise,* December 1, 1904; *Moman Pruiett, Criminal Lawyer,* author uncertain, pp. 179-83.

10. *Moman Pruiett, Criminal Lawyer,* author uncertain, pp. 106-8.

11. *Atoka Citizen,* March 28, 1907.

12. *Cherokee* (OK) *Republican,* September 30, 1910.

13. This hanging occurred at Ada, Oklahoma, on April 19, 1909. The incident is thoroughly covered in *Shotgun for Hire*, by Glenn Shirley, University of Oklahoma Press, Norman, 1970, and *Four Men Hanging*, by Welborn Hope, Century Press, Oklahoma City, 1974.

14. *Daily Oklahoman*, February 5, 1909.

15. Ibid., September 6, 1912.

16. Ibid., February 7, 1914.

17. *Waurika Democrat*, May 3, 1918.

18. *Daily Oklahoman*, September 13, 1920.

19. Ibid., October 10, 1921.

20. Ibid., October 12, 1921.

21. *Oklahoma News*, October 12, 1921.

22. Ibid., January 27, 1922.

23. Ibid., July 17, 1923.

24. *Oklahoma City Times*, September 20, 1927.

25. Ibid., February 19, 1934.

26. Ibid., February 28, 1935.

27. Ibid., July 2, 1935.

28. Copy of Moman Pruiett's death certificate.

29. *Daily Oklahoman*, December 19, 1945. Some of the articles and information for this chapter were provided the author by Richard Jones of Oklahoma City.

Chapter 22: Wes Hudson: Had Gun, Did Travel

1. *Daily Oklahoman*, May 27, 1906.

2. The family and early life of Little Wes is based on information provided to the author by Fred Hudson of Harrison, Arkansas. The current Fred Hudson is a nephew of Little Wes. Until recent years, Fred was unaware that his uncle had also been known as "Fred."

3. *Stillwater Advance*, December 26, 1901.

4. *Marshall* (AR) *Mountain Wave*, February 28, 1903.

5. "Little Wes Hudson, from the Innocent Sunbeam, to the Instrument of Death," by Sammie Rose and Pat Wood, in the May 1991 issue of *True West* magazine.

6. *Marshall* (AR) *Mountain Wave,* March 28, 1903.

7. Ibid., September 19, 1903.

8. *Ozarks Mountaineer,* Vol. 27, No. 243.

9. Compiled from several clippings of articles of which neither the newspaper names nor the dates were identified.

10. *True West,* May 1991.

11. *Shawnee News* (dateline Little Rock, AR), June 22, 1905.

12. *True West,* May 1991.

13. (Little Rock) *Arkansas Gazette,* May 24, 1906.

14. *Anadarko Daily Democrat,* May 24, 1906.

Chapter 23: Lute Houston's Murder Trials

1. *Apache* (OK) *Weekly Review,* May 11, 1906.

2. *West of Hell's Fringe,* by Glenn Shirley, University of Oklahoma Press, Norman, 1978, pp. 413, 422.

3. *Daily Oklahoman,* September 18, 1932.

4. *Hobart News-Republican,* May 17, 1906.

5. Ibid., May 18, 1906.

6. Ibid., May 25, 1906.

7. *Daily Oklahoman,* September 18, 1932.

8. An undated note from Bernice Hawkins, Kiowa County deputy court clerk, in reponse to the author's letter of inquiry, dated April 5, 1993.

9. Additional information about Al Jennings may be found in the book *West of Hell's Fringe,* by Glenn Shirley.

10. *Sunday Oklahoman,* November 8, 1987.

Chapter 24: Showdown in an Anadarko Saloon

1. The author requested information from the appropriate records offices in Texas and Oklahoma about Jim Bourland's being in prison. Neither state has confirmed that he was confined in its prison system.

2. *Daily Oklahoman,* September 18, 1932.

3. *Andarko Daily Democrat,* May 24, 1906.

4. Ibid.

5. *Daily Oklahoman,* May 26, 1906.

6. Letter from Debbie Riddle, Anadarko Chamber of Commerce, to the author, dated January 26, 1994.

7. *Daily Oklahoman,* May 26, 1906.

8. Letter to the author from Fred Hudson, nephew of Wesley "Fred" Hudson, dated April 20, 1994.

9. *Daily Oklahoman,* September 18, 1932.

Chapter 25: "Hookey" Miller, a Man to Reckon With

1. Family information provided by Helen (Miller) Gaines, granddaughter of George D. "Hookey" Miller; copy of Texas Ranger discharge papers.

2. These crimes and the criminal career of George "Red Buck" Weightman are covered more completely in the books *West of Hell's Fringe,* by Glenn Shirley, University of Oklahoma Press, Norman, 1978, and *In Pursuit of the Outlaw, Red Buck,* by Charles Rainbolt, private printing, no city, undated.

3. *Oklahoma State Capital,* March 21, 1896; letter from Chris Madsen to Zoe Tilghman, dated October 24, 1936.

4. *Arapaho Argus,* February 20, 1896. Jim Harbolt was a fugitive from Texas who was wanted for the murder of Hemphill County sheriff T.T. McGee.

5. *Arapaho Bee,* June 23, 1922.

6. *Arapaho Argus,* March 5, 1896.

7. Ibid. Canute was originally known as "Oak." Joe Ventioner recovered from his wound and lived for many years.

8. *El Reno Globe,* April 17, 1896.

9. *Arapaho Bee,* October 23, 1896.

10. Letter to the author from the Texas Department of Criminal Justice, Institutional Division, dated March 11, 1993.

11. Copy of letter from Jesse W. Couch, Matador, Texas, dated July 21, 1964, to Mr. and Mrs. G.D. Miller (George Jr.); *Clinton Daily News,* November 28, 1993.

12. The notorious saloon brought into being a small town, with a post

office from 1903 to 1907, which was named Corner.

13. *Shawnee News,* October 14, 1904; *Hobart Republican,* November 22, 1906; letter to the author from Helen Gaines, dated December 3, 1993.

14. *Shawnee News,* July 7,10,11, 1905.

15. Ibid., July 23,29, 1905.

16. *Hobart Republican,* November 22, 1906.

17. *Clinton Daily News,* November 28, 1993, a full-page article about Hookey Miller that was based on information provided by his grand-daughters, Helen Gaines, daughter of George Miller Jr., and Georgia Phillips, daughter of Ed Miller.

18. Letter to the author from Helen Gaines, dated January 17, 1994.

19. *Perry Republican,* July 26, 1923.

20. *Blackwell Daily Tribune,* August 5, 1923.

21. (Newkirk) *Republican News,* July 27, 1923; *Oklahoma City Times,* July 24, 1923.

22. *Perry Republican,* July 26, 1923.

23. *Blackwell Daily Tribune,* September 29, 1923.

Chapter 26: Still More Trouble for the Hughes Brothers

1. *Daily Oklahoman,* September 4, 1932.

2. *Arapho Bee,* March 27, 1908.

3. Ibid., November 27, 1908.

4. Ibid., July 23, 1909.

5. Ibid., July 30, 1909.

6. Ibid., November 18, 1910.

7. Ibid., December 9, 1910.

8. Ibid., December 30, 1910.

9. Ibid., February 3, 1911.

10. Letter to the author from Records Division, Oklahoma Department of Corrections, dated September 22, 1993.

11. Letter to the author from U.S. Department of Justice, dated May 19, 1994, including sixty-four pages of Jim Hughes' prison record.

12. *Daily Oklahoman,* September 18, 1932.

Chapter 27: The Next Generation

1. *Cordell Beacon,* September 8, 1910.

2. *Arapaho Bee,* September 16, 1910.

3. *Cordell Beacon,* September 8, 1910.

4. *Oklahoma City Times,* October 23, 1910.

5. *Clinton Chronicle,* October 26, 1920.

6. Letter to the author, dated December 22, 1993, from Records Division, Oklahoma Department of Corrections, with copies of inmate cards.

7. *Cordell Beacon,* August 12, 1926.

8. Letter from Oklahoma Department of Corrections, dated December 22, 1993.

9. *Cordell Beacon,* August 12, 1926. In this article Ben Jr. is referred to as "Raleigh Hughes."

10. Ibid., October 21, 1926.

11. Ibid., December 26, 1926.

12. Copy of Ben Hughes Jr.'s prison inmate record card.

13. *Cordell Beacon,* December 27, 1928.

14. Copy of Ben Hughes, Jr.'s prison inmate record card.

15. *Cordell Beacon,* December 27, 1928.

16. *Cheyenne Star,* September 22, 1932.

17. Copy of Ben Hughes Jr.'s prison inmate record card.

18. Copy of Ben Hughes' death certificate.

Index

227